871 FAMOUS LAST WORDS

and Put-downs, Insults, Squelches,
Compliments, Rejoinders, Epigrams,
and Epitaphs of Famous People

GYLES BRANDRETH

BELL PUBLISHING COMPANY
NEW YORK

This 1982 edition is published by Bell Publishing Company,
distributed by Crown Publishers, Inc.,
by arrangement with Sterling Publishing Co., Inc.

Previously published as *The Last Word*.

Manufactured in the United States of America

Library of Congress Cataloging in Publication Data

Brandreth, Gyles Daubeney, 1948–
   871 famous last words.

   Previous ed. published as: The last word. c1979.
   1. Last words.   2. Invective.   3. Epitaphs.
I. Title.   II. Title: Eight hundred seventy-one famous last
words.
PN6328.L3B7 1982   808.88′2   82-9574

ISBN: 0-517-383497
h g f e d c b

Contents

First Words

The last earthly words of the great German composer Ludwig van Beethoven were either:
"I shall hear in Heaven."
or:
"Too bad, too bad! It's too late!"
or:
"Friends applaud, the Comedy is over."
But which of the three they were I simply can't tell you.
You see, I wasn't there. Indeed I've not been present when
any of the final utterances featured in this book were origi-
nally spoken. All the same, while I can't put my hand on my
heart and swear that the words I have quoted were without
exception the actual final words of the various people to
whom they are attributed, I have done my best to put the
right last words into the right mouths at the right time.

Given the millions of people who have lived since the
dawn of mankind and given that everyone who can speak
will come up with Last Words of a sort, choosing the ones to
include here hasn't been an easy task. The last words of
many of the most famous and interesting and important
figures of history were simply never recorded, while many
of those that were recorded are often of such a bleak ba-
nality as to be really of no interest at all.

The ones I have chosen are included either because I
found them striking or touching or witty or apt or because

the person who uttered these last words was of such stature that almost anything said is of some significance. When I've been faced with alternative last words for the same person I have either included more than one possibility so that you can decide which you think *ought* to have been their last words or I have selected the ones that research suggests actually *were* their last words and omitted the alternatives. And when I have come across more than one claimant for a particular set of last words, I've tended to drop the last words altogether. For example, at least six people are reputed to have said to the clergyman who was at their deathbed and asked them to renounce the devil and all his works, "This is no time for making enemies!"

All in all I've done my best to produce a collection of quotations that can genuinely lay claim to being The Last Word in last words of the famous. And if I have made any mistakes I trust the ghosts of those I have wronged will make themselves known to me—either in this world or the next.

—Gyles Brandreth

I
Last
Words

Pierre Abelard (1097–1142), French theologian and philospher, famous for his love affair with Héloise:
"I don't know. I don't know!"

Abigail Adams (1744–1818), wife of the second President:
"Do not grieve, my friend—my dearest friend. I am ready to go, and John it will not be long."

John Adams (1735–1826), unaware of the irony that Jefferson's death had preceded his own by a few hours:
"Thomas Jefferson still survives."

Jane Addams (1860–1935), social reformer and campaigner for temperance. When offered spirits to revive her:
"Always, always water for me."

Joseph Addison (1672–1719), British man of letters and poet:
"See in what peace a Christian may die."

Agrippina (15–59 A.D.), mother of the Emperor Nero. To the assassins sent by her son:
"Smite my womb."

Albert, Prince Consort (1819–61), husband to Queen Victoria. To the Queen:

"You have not forgotten the important communication to Nemours? Good little woman."

Thomas B. Aldrich (1836–1907), poet and novelist:

"In spite of it all, I am going to sleep."

Alexander the Great (356–323 B.C.). Asked who was to succeed him:

"The strongest."

Alexander I (1777–1825), Czar of Russia:

"What a beautiful day."

Alexander VI (1431?–1503), Pope, Roderigo Borgia:

"I come. It is right. Wait a minute."

Alfred the Great (849–901), King of Wessex, England:

"I desire to leave to the men that come after me a remembrance of me in good works."

Ethan Allen (1738–89), officer during the American Revolution. On being told that the angels were waiting for him:

"Waiting are they, waiting are they? Well, let 'em wait!"

Albert Anastasia (d. 1957), gangster. On being shot while in a barber's chair:

"Haircut!"

John André (1751–80), British spy executed during the American Revolution. Hoping to be shot, he was dismayed at the sight of the hangman's noose:

"I am reconciled to my death but I detest the mode."
Later he added:
"It will be but a momentary pang. I pray you bear witness that I met my fate like a brave man."

Mark Antony (83–30 B.C.). Defeated by Octavius at Actium and having inflicted his suicide blow, he was carried to Cleopatra:

"You must not pity me in this last turn of fate. You should rather be happy in the remembrance of our love and in the recollection that of all men I was once the most powerful and now at the end have fallen not dishonourably, a Roman by a Roman vanquished."

Pietro Aretino (1492–1557), Italian comic dramatist and poet. After receiving the last rites:

"Keep the rats away now that I am all greased up."

Lewis A. Arminstead (1817–63), Confederate general. Storming Union artillery on foot, his ammunition spent, he exhorted his men to advance:

"Give them the cold steel, men!"

Atahualpa (1500?–33), last of the Incas. On being condemned to death by burning, he said to Pizarro:

"What have I done, or my children, that I should meet such a fate? And from your hands too you, who have met with friendship and kindness from my people, who have received nothing but benefits from my hands."

Caesar Augustus (63 B.C.–14 A.D.), first Emperor of Rome:
"Forty young men are carrying me off."

Marcus Aurelius (121–180), last of the great Antonine emperors of Rome. Conscious of his approaching death, he directed an official enquiry to his successor:
"Go to the rising star, for I am setting."

Jane Austen (1775–1817), novelist. Asked if she required anything:
"Nothing but death."

Stephen F. Austin (1793–1836), Texas founder:
"Texas recognized! Archer told me so. Did you see it in the papers?"

Francis Bacon (1561–1626), English philosopher and statesman:
"My name and memory I leave to man's charitable speeches, to foreign nations and to the next age."

Max Baer (1909–59), World Heavyweight Boxing Champion:
"Oh, God, here I go!"

Norman Baesell (d. 1944), Air Force major. Flying the aircraft in which bandleader Glenn Miller disappeared over the English Channel:
"What's the matter, Miller, do you want to live forever?"

Jean Sylvain Bailly (1736–93), mayor of Paris at the beginning of the French Revolution. Approaching the scaffold a voice in the crowd called out to him:

"Thou tremblest, Bailly."

"I am cold, my friend," was his reply.

Arizona "Ma" Barker (d. 1935), bank robber. Giving the order to her sons to start the fatal shootout with the FBI:

"All right! Go ahead!"

Barney Barnato (1852–97), South African millionaire. Before jumping over the side of a ship:

"What is the time?"

Phineas T. Barnum (1810–91), impresario and showman:

"How were the circus receipts tonight at Madison Square Garden?"

Sir James M. Barrie (1860–1937), playwright, creator of "Peter Pan":

"I can't sleep."

Clarence Walker Barron (1855–1928), publisher of the "Wall Street Journal":

"What's the news?"

John Barrymore (1882–1942), actor. To his old friend Gene Fowler:

"Tell me, Gene, is it true that you're the illegitimate son of Buffalo Bill?"

Louis Barthou (1862–1934), French politician. Assassinated with King Alexander I of Yugoslavia:

"I can't see what's happening now. My eyeglasses, where are my eyeglasses?"

Clara Barton (1821–1912), founder of the American Red Cross:

"Let me go, let me go."

Pierre du Terrail, Chevalier de Bayard (1476–1524), "the knight without fear and without reproach." To the Genoese rebel who offered him commiseration:

"Pity me not: I die as a man of honour ought, in the discharge of my duty: they indeed are objects of pity who fight against their king, their country and their oath."

"God and my country!"

Saint Thomas Becket (1118–70), Archbishop of Canterbury and martyr. To the assassins:

"I am prepared to die for Christ and for His Church. I charge you in the name of the Almighty not to hurt any other person here, for none of them have been concerned in the late transactions."

The Venerable Bede (673–735), English teacher and theologian. Dictating a translation of St. John's gospel, his scribe said to him:

"Dearest master, there is only one sentence left to write."

"Write it quickly."

"It is finished now."

"Thou hast well said, 'All is finished now.' Glory to Thee O God, Father, Son, and Holy Ghost."

Henry Ward Beecher (1813–87), Congregationalist preacher:

"Now comes the mystery."

Sir Max Beerbohm (1872–1956), English writer and caricaturist. Asked whether he had had a good sleep:
"No. Thanks for everything."

Ludwig van Beethoven (1770–1827):
"Friends applaud, the Comedy is over."

Alexander Graham Bell (1847–1922). When asked not to hurry his dictation:
"But I have to. So little done. So much to do!"

Arnold Bennett (1867–1931), British novelist:
"Everything has gone wrong, my girl."

Jeremy Bentham (1748–1832), English political theorist:
"I now feel that I am dying. Our care must be to minimize pain. Do not let the servants come into the room and keep away the youths. It will be distressing to them and they can be of no service."

Hector Berlioz (1803–69), French composer:
"One thousand greetings to Balakirev."

Ryumin Michael Bestuzhev (d. 1826), Russian revolutionary, after the first rope had broken:
"Nothing succeeds with me. Even here I meet with disappointment."

Billy the Kid (1859–81), outlaw (William Bonney), to Pat Garrett, who killed him:
"Who's there?"

Armand Louis de Gontaut, Duc de Lauzun, Duc de Biron (1749–93). At the guillotine, to the executioner:

"I beg a thousand pardons, my friend, but permit me to finish this last dozen of oysters!"

On the scaffold:

"I have been false to my God, my order and my King. I die full of faith and repentance."

Prince Otto von Bismarck (1851–98). To his daughter who was attending him:

"Thanks, my child."

"Dear Lord, I believe. Help Thou my unbelief and receive me into Thy heavenly Kingdom."

Nicholas Boileau (1636–1711), French critic. To a playwright who was trying to persuade him to read his latest work:

"Do you wish to hasten my last hour?"

Anne Boleyn (1507–36), second Queen of King Henry VIII of England:

"The executioner is, I believe, an expert . . . and my neck is very slender. Oh God, have pity on my soul, O God have pity on my soul . . ."

Simón Bolívar (1783–1830), South American liberator. Dying in Colombia:

"Let us go—let us go—these people don't want us in this land! Let us go, boys.—Take my luggage on board the frigate."

Elisa Bonaparte (1777–1820), sister of Napoleon. On being told that nothing was as certain as death:

"Except taxes."

Napoleon Bonaparte (1769–1821):
"France! Army! Head of the Army! Josephine!"

John Wilkes Booth (1838–65), assassin of Abraham Lincoln:
"Tell my mother I died for my country . . . I thought I did for the best . . . Useless! Useless!"

Saint Carlo Borromeo (1538–84), cardinal and Archbishop of Milan. Asked when he wished to receive the viaticum:
"At once."

Dominique Bouhors (d. 1702), French grammarian:
"I am about to, or, I am going to die. Either expression is used."

Andrew Bradford (d. 1742), publisher of the first newspaper in Philadelphia:
"Oh Lord, forgive the errata!"

Johannes Brahms (1833–97), after finishing a glass of wine:
"Ah, that tastes nice, thank you."

Charlotte Brontë (1816–55), English novelist:
"Oh, I am not going to die, am I? He will not separate us, we have been so happy!"

Rupert Brooke (1887–1915), English poet:
"Hullo."

John Brown (1800–59), antislavery campaigner. Asked on the scaffold if he was tired:
"No, but don't keep me waiting longer than necessary."

Elizabeth Barrett Browning (1806–61), English poetess. Asked how she was feeling:
  "Beautiful."

Marcus Junius Brutus (85–42 B.C.), conspirator against Caius Julius Caesar. Killed at the battle of Philippi:
  "Oh wretched valour thou wert but a name, and yet I worshipped thee as real indeed. But now it seems thou wert but fortune's slave."

Buddha (*c.* 500–*c.* 420 B.C.):
  "O Ananda! Do not weep. Have I not told you that we must part from all we hold most dear and pleasant? . . . persevere and you too shall be quite free from this thirst of life, this chain of ignorance."
  "Work out your salvation with diligence."

Hans Guido von Bülow (1830–94), German pianist and conductor. Asked how he was feeling:
  "Bad."

Ferruccio Busoni (1866–1924), Italian pianist and composer. To his wife:
  "Dear Gerda, I thank you for every day we have been together."

Samuel Butler (1835–1902), English writer:
  "Have you brought the cheque-book, Alfred?"

George Gordon Noel (Lord) **Byron** (1788–1824):
  "The damned doctors have drenched me so that I can scarcely stand. I want to sleep now. Shall I sue for mercy? Come, come, no weakness. Let me be a man to the last."

Saint Frances Xavier Cabrini (1850–1917), the first American saint:
"Bring me anything you like. If I don't take it I may take something else."

Caius Julius Caesar (*c.* 100–44 B.C.):
"Et tu Brute?"

John C. Calhoun (1782–1850), Senator and champion of the South:
"The South! The poor South! God knows what will become of her."

Caligula (12–41), Emperor of Rome:
"I am still alive!"

Luiz vax de Camoens (1524–80), Portuguese poet:
"I am happy that I die in the bosom of my country—nay, in that I am dying with her."

Sir Henry Campbell-Bannerman (1836–1908), British Prime Minister:
"This is not the end of me."

Thomas Carlyle (1795–1881), British historian:
"So this is death—well . . ."

Andrew Carnegie (1835–1919), steel magnate and philanthropist. To his wife who had wished him a good night:
"I hope so."

Lewis Carroll (1832–98), English mathematician (*nom de plume* of C. L. Dodgson), creator of "Alice in Wonderland":
"Take away those pillows—I shall need them no more."

Kit Carson (1809–68), trapper and hunter:
"Adios, compadre!"

Enrico Caruso (1873–1921), Italian operatic tenor:
"Doro, I can't breathe!"

Phoebe Cary (1824–71), poetess. Quoting herself:
"One sweetly solemn thought
Comes to me o'er and o'er
I am nearer to home today
Than I have ever been before."

Giacomo Casanova de Seingalt (1725–98), Italian adventurer and lover:
"I have lived as a philosopher. I die as a Christian."

Edith Cavell (1895–1915), British nurse. Executed by a German firing squad for helping Allied troops escape from Belgium:
"I realize that patriotism is not enough. I must have no hatred or bitterness towards anyone."

Neville Chamberlain (1869–1940), British politician and Prime Minister:
"Approaching dissolution brings relief."

Marshal Pierre Chambronne (d. 1815), Commander of the Old Guard, at Waterloo. Refusing to surrender:
"Merde! The Old Guard dies but does not yield!"

Gerald Chapman (d. 1926), conman, murderer, swindler. Executed for killing a policeman:
"Death itself isn't dreadful, but hanging seems an awkward way of entering the adventure."

Charles I (1600–49), **King of England. On the scaffold:**
"I lay not my blood on you, or on my people, and demand no other compensation for any punishment than the return of peace and a revival of the fidelity which the kingdom owes to my children.

"My friend, I go from a corruptible crown to an incorruptible."

To Bishop Juxon:
"Remember."

Charles II (1630–85), **King of England. Referring to his mistress, Nell Gwyn:**
"Let not poor Nelly starve."

Anton Pavlovich Chekhov (1860–1904), **Russian playwright. Permitted a glass of champagne by his doctor:**
"I am dying . . . I haven't drunk champagne for a long time."

Gilbert Keith Chesterton (1874–1936), **English critic, novelist and poet:**
"The issue now is clear: it is between light and darkness and everyone must choose his side."

Chuang Tzu (4th century B.C.), **Chinese philosopher of Taoism. Asked about the manner of his burial:**
"Above ground, I shall be food for the kites; below I shall be food for mole, crickets and ants. Why rob the one to feed the other?"

Sir Winston Churchill (1874–1965), **British statesman:**
"Oh, I am so bored with it all."

Ike Clanton (d. 1881), rancher. Gunned down by the Earp brothers in the gunfight at the OK Corral:

"God, God, won't somebody give me some more cartridges for a last shot . . ?"

Henry Clay (1777–1852), statesman and orator:

"I believe, my son, that I am going. Now I lay me down to sleep."

Georges Clemenceau (1841–1929), French statesman and premier:

"I wish to be buried standing—facing Germany."

Grover Cleveland (1837–1908), 22nd U.S. President:

"I have tried so hard to do right."

"Buffalo Bill" Cody (1846–1917), showman and folk hero:

"Well, let's forget about it and play High Five. I wish Johnny would come."

Charles Coffin (d. 1916), war correspondent:

"If it were not for this pain I should get up and write."

Sidonie Gabrielle Colette (1873–1954), French novelist:

"To reach completion is to return to one's starting point. My instinctive bent which takes pleasure in curves and spheres and circles."

Samuel Colt (1814–62), arms manufacturer and inventor:

"It's all over now."

Christopher Columbus (1451–1506):

"Into thy hands, O Lord, I commend my spirit."

Confucius (551–478 B.C.):
"I am a man of Yin and the last night I dreamt that I was sitting with offerings before me between two great pillars. No intelligent monarch arises; there is not one in the empire that will make me his master. My time is come to die."

Jay Cooke (1821–1905), banker. Hearing the reading of a prayer for the dead:
"That was the right prayer."

Calvin Coolidge (1872–1933), 29th U.S. President:
"Good morning, Robert."

Jean Baptiste Camille Corot (1796–1875), French painter:
"In spite of myself I go on hoping—I hope with all my heart there will be painting in heaven."

Sir Noel Coward (1899–1973), English actor and dramatist:
"Good night, my darlings, I'll see you in the morning."

Bernard Coy (d. 1946), murderer. Shot attempting to escape from Alcatraz:
"It doesn't matter. I figure I licked the Rock anyway."

Hart Crane (1899–1932), poet. Jumping off ship:
"Goodbye, everybody!"

Stephen Crane (1871–1900), author of "The Red Badge of Courage":
"Robert—when you come to the hedge—that we all must go over—it isn't so bad. You feel sleepy—and you don't care. Just a little dreamy anxiety—which world you're really in— that's all."

Thomas Cranmer (1489–1556), Archbishop of Canterbury. Burning at the stake, he held his right hand in the flames to burn first:

"This hand having sinned in signing the writing must be the first to suffer punishment. This hand hath offended."

F. Marion Crawford (1854–1909), novelist:

"I love to see the reflection of the sun in the bookcase."

Oliver Cromwell (1599–1658), Lord Protector of England:

"My desire is to make what haste I may to be gone."

Bing Crosby (1904–77), singer and movie star:

"That was a great game of golf, fellers."

James Cross (1821–90), Scottish physicist. After a life of abstention, he requests spirits on his deathbed:

"I'll take a wee drop of that. I don't think there's much fear of me learning to drink now."

Isapwo Mukiska Crowfoot (d. 1850), Chief of the Blackfoot Confederacy:

"A little while and I will be gone from among you, whither I cannot tell. From nowhere we came, into nowhere we go. What is life? It is a flash of a firefly in the night. It is a breath of a buffalo in the winter time. It is as the little shadow that runs across the grass and loses itself in the sunset."

Francis "Two Gun" Crowley (d. 1931), bank robber and murderer. Sentenced to death by electrocution:

"You sons of bitches. Give my love to mother."

Bood (Boudinet) Crumpton (d. 1875), outlaw. Executed for committing a murder while intoxicated:

". . . men, the next time you lift a glass of whiskey, I want you to look into the bottom of the glass and see if there isn't a hangman's noose in it, like the one here."

e. e. cummings (1894–1962), painter and poet. Told by his wife to stop cutting wood on such a hot day:

"I'm going to stop now, but I'm going to sharpen the axe before I put it up, dear."

Lady Emerald Cunard (d. 1948), socialite. Offered a teaspoon of champagne by her maid, she refused it:

"No. Open a bottle for the nurse and yourself."

Marie Curie (1867–1934), scientist. Offered a pain-killing injection:

"I don't want it."

John Philpot Curran (1750–1817), Irish writer and orator. To his doctor, who told him he was coughing with "more difficulty":

"That is surprising, since I have been practising all night."

Cyrus the Great (601–c. 538 B.C.), founder of the Persian Empire. From his farewell address, recorded by Xenophon:

"I can never be persuaded that the soul lives on longer than it dwells in this mortal body and that it dies on its separation . . . Remember this as my last and dying words. If you do kindness to your friends, you will be able to injure your enemies. Farewell."

Leon Czolgosz (d. 1901), assassin of President McKinley:

"I killed the President because he was the enemy of the good people, the working people. I am not sorry for my crime."

Joseph de Veuster Damian (1840–1889), priest, who devoted 25 years as a missionary to helping the lepers of Molokai, Hawaii, before dying of the disease himself. To one of his companions, who requested that he be left the father's mantle, as Elisha was left Elijah's:

"Why, what would you do with it? It is full of leprosy.

"Well! God's will be done. He knows best. My work, with all its faults and failures, is in His hands and before Easter I shall see my Saviour."

Charles Darwin (1809–82), English naturalist:

"I am not in the least afraid to die."

David (d. 1015 B.C.), King of Israel. To Solomon:

"Be strong and of good courage and do it; fear not, nor be dismayed: for the Lord, even my God, will be with thee: He will not fail thee, till thou hast finished all the work for the service of the house of the Lord."

Jefferson Davis (1808–89), President of the Confederacy. Offered a dose of medicine:

"Please excuse me, I cannot take it."

Daniel Defoe (1660–1731), English writer, author of "Robinson Crusoe":

"I do not know which is the more difficult in a Christian life, to live well or to die well."

René Descartes (1596–1650), French philosopher and mathematician:

"My soul, thou hast long been held captive. The hour had come for thee to quit thy prison, to leave the trammels of this body. Then to this separation with joy and courage."

Charles Dickens (1812–70), English novelist. To his sister-in-law and friends trying to help him to a couch:

"On the ground."

Emily Dickinson (1830–86), poet:

"I must go in, the fog is rising."
When offered a glass of water:
"Oh, is that all it is?"

Denis Diderot (1713–84), French philosopher. Accepting an apricot, offered by his wife:

"But what the devil do you think that will do to me?"

Diogenes the Cynic (412–323 B.C.). Greek philosopher:

Xeniades:	"How do you want to be buried?"
Diogenes:	"Face downwards."
Xeniades:	"Why?"
Diogenes:	"Because everything will shortly be turned upside down."

Benjamin Disraeli (1804–81), British Prime Minister:

"I had rather live, but I am not afraid to die."

John Donne (1572–1631), British poet and clergyman:

"I were miserable if I might not die. Thy Kingdom come, Thy Will be done."

Frederick Douglass (1817–95), campaigner for Black rights:
   "Why, what does this mean?"

Paul Doumer (1857–1932), President of France. Believing that he had been hit by a car, not by an assassin's bullet:
   "Ah, a road accident . . . a road accident."

Anthony J. Drexel III (d. 1893), socialite. Demonstrating a new pistol, he accidentally shot himself:
   "Here's one you've never seen before . . ."

John Baptiste Dubois (1670–1742), French diplomat and divine:
   "Death is a law and not a punishment. Three things ought to console us for giving up life: the friends whom we have lost, the few persons worthy of being loved whom we leave behind us, and finally the memory of our stupidities and the assurance that they are now going to stop."

Isadora Duncan (1878–1927), dancer:
   "Adieu my friends, I go on to glory!"

Eleanora Duse (1859–1924), actress:
   "We must stir ourselves. Move on! Work! Work! Cover me! Must move on! Must work! Cover me!"

Joseph Duveen (1869–1939), English art dealer. After living beyond all medical prognoses:
   "Well, I fooled them for five years."

Jeanne Eagels (1894–1929), actress:
   "I'm going to Dr. Caldwell's for one of my regular treatments."

Morgan Earp (d. 1882), lawman. Dying in the OK Corral, he finally agreed with his brother's views on the afterlife:
"I guess you were right, Wyatt. I can't see a damn thing."

George Eastman (1854–1932), philanthropist and inventor of photographic equipment. Died by his own hand:
"To my friends: my work is done. Why wait?"

Thomas Alva Edison (1847–1931), inventor:
"It's very beautiful over there."

Colonel Henry Egbert (d. 1899), killed during the invasion of Manila:
"Goodbye, General. I'm done. I'm too old."

George Eliot (*nom de plume* of **Marian Evans**) (1819–80), English novelist:
"Tell them I have a great pain in the left side."

Elizabeth I (1533–1603), Queen of England:
"All my possessions for a moment of time."

Ralph Waldo Emerson (1803–82), to Bronson Alcott:
"Goodbye, my friend."

Empedocles (490–430 B.C.), Greek philosopher:
"I am your deathless god: a mortal never more."

Epicurus (341–270 B.C.), Greek philosopher:
"Now farewell, remember all my works."

Desiderius Erasmus (1466–1536), Dutch humanist:
"Dear God!"

William Etty (1787–1849), British painter:
"Wonderful, wonderful this death."

Daniel Evans (1854–75), murderer. Surveying the crowd at his execution:
"There are worse men here than me."

Douglas Fairbanks, Sr. (1883–1939), actor:
"I've never felt better!"

François Felix Faure (1841–99), French statesman:
"You see, my poor Bridier, what a poor thing man is, even when he is President of the Republic."

Kathleen Ferrier (1912–53), English opera singer:
"Now I'll have *eine kleine* pause."

Paddy Finucane (d. 1940), British Royal Air Force pilot:
"This is it, chaps."

Adolf Fischer (d. 1881), Haymarket rioter. On being hanged:
"This is the happiest moment of my life!"

F. Scott Fitzgerald (1896–1940), writer. To Sheilah Graham, shortly before collapsing unconscious in the garden of a Hollywood hotel:

Fitzgerald: "I'm going to Schwab's to get some ice cream."

Graham: "But you might miss the doctor—if it's something sweet you want, I've got some Hershey bars."

Fitzgerald: "Good enough. They'll be fine."

Charles "Pretty Boy" Floyd (d. 1934), bank robber. Surrounded by the F.B.I. in Ohio:
"Who the hell tipped you off? I'm Floyd all right. You got me this time."

Ferdinand Foch (1851–1929), French Marshal:
"Let me go."

Bernard de Fontenelle (1657–1757), French scholar:
"I feel nothing except a certain difficulty in continuing to exist."

Andrew Hull Foote (1806–63), American admiral:
"We will have them, North and South. The colored people, yes, we will have them. We must have charity, charity, charity . . ."

Stephen C. Foster (1826–64), American composer:
"Dear friends and gentle hearts."

George Fox (1624–90), founder of the Quakers:
"Never heed, the Lord's presence is over all weakness and death; the Lord reigns, blessed be the Lord."

Anatole France (1844–1924), French man of letters:
"Maman."

Saint Francis of Assisi (1182–1226):
"Farewell, my children; remain always in the fear of the Lord. That temptation and tribulation which is to come, is now at hand and happy shall they be who persevere in the good they have begun. I hasten to go to our Lord, to whose grace I recommend you.

"Bring my soul out of prison that I may praise Thy name: the just wait for me till Thou reward me."

Hans Frank (1900–46), Nazi war criminal:
"A thousand years will pass and the guilt of Germany will not be erased."

Franz Josef (1830–1916), Emperor of Austria. Singing while dying:
"God preserve the emperor."

Frederick the Great (1712–86), King of Prussia. To the sun:
"Perhaps I shall be nearer thee soon!"
"We are over the hill, we shall go better now."

Frederick William I (1688–1740), King of Prussia. Hearing the passage from the Book of Job, "Naked I came into the world and naked shall go," he answered:
"No, not quite naked; I shall have my uniform on."
"Herr Jesu, to Thee I live; Herr Jesu, to Thee I die: in life and death, Thou art my gain."

Henry Clay Frick (1849–1919), industrialist:
"That will be all; now I think I'll go to sleep."

Charles Frohman (d. 1915), theatrical producer. Drowned when the *Lusitania* was sunk:
"Why fear death? It is the most beautiful adventure in life."

Thomas Gainsborough (1727–88), English painter:
"We are all going to Heaven and Van Dyck is of the company."

Galileo Galilei (1564–1642), Italian astronomer:
"Yet it still moves."

John Galsworthy (1867–1933), English novelist and playwright:
"I have enjoyed too pleasant circumstances."

Mohandas Karamchand Gandhi (1869–1948), Indian statesman:
"Oh, God."

James Garfield (1831–81), 20th U.S. President, assassinated:
"The people my trust."

Giuseppe Garibaldi (1807–82), Italian patriot. Indicating a pair of finches perched on the window-sill:
"Maybe they are the souls of my little ones come to call me. Feed them when I am gone."

David Garrick (1717–79), English actor. To his servant:
"Well, Tom, I shall do very well yet and make you amends for all this trouble."

André Gide (1869–1951), French writer:
"*C'est bien.*"

Sir Humphrey Gilbert (1835–83), English explorer and navigator. As his ship was sinking, he rallied his crew:
"Courage, my lads! We are as near to heaven by sea as by land."

Gary Gilmore (d. 1977), murderer. Executed by firing squad:
"Let's do it."

George Gipp (d. 1920), football star. Last request to Knute Rockne:

"One day when the going is tough and a big game is hanging in the balance, ask the team to win one for the Gipper. I don't know where I'll be, Rock, but I'll know about it, and I'll be happy."

Joseph Goebbels (1897–1945), Nazi politician. To his adjutant:

"Schwaegermann, this is the worst treachery of all. The generals have betrayed the Fuehrer. Everything is lost. I shall die with my wife and family. You will burn our bodies Can you do that?"

Johann Wolfgang von Goethe (1749–1832). German romantic poet:

"More light! More light!"

Nikolai Gogol (1809–52), Russian novelist:

"And I shall laugh a bitter laugh."

Oliver Goldsmith (1728–74), English writer. Asked by his doctor whether his mind was at ease, he replied:

"No, it is not."

Charles "Chinese" Gordon (1833–85), British general. Killed at Khartoum:

"Where is the Mahdi?"

Santa Maria Goretti (d. 1902), murdered at age 11 while resisting the advances of a 19-year-old youth:

"May God forgive him; I want him in heaven."

Ulysses S. Grant (1822–85), 18th U.S. President:
"I am a great sufferer all the time . . . all that I can do is pray that the prayers of all these good people may be answered so far as to have us all meet in another and better world. I cannot speak even in a whisper."

Horace Greeley (1811–72), publisher, editor and founder of the New York "Tribune":
"It is done."

Joseph Green (d. 1863), surgeon. Checking his own pulse:
"Congestion . . . stopped."

Edvard Grieg (1843–1907), Norwegian composer:
"Well, if it must be so."

Seaman Grontoft (d. 1922), Norwegian wireless operator. Signaling the rescue ship:
"We are sinking stern first. The boats are smashed. Can't hold out longer. The skipper dictated that. He ought to know. Where did I put my hat? Sorry we couldn't wait for you. Pressing business elsewhere. Skaal."

Joseph J. Gurney (1788–1847), English Quaker, philanthropist. To his wife:
"I think I feel a little joyful, dearest."

Fitz-Greene Halleck (1790–1867), poet. To his sister:
"Maria, hand me my pantaloons, if you please."

Richard Halliburton (1900–39), writer, explorer and adventurer. Final signal sent from his ship sinking in the Pacific:
"Southerly gales, squalls, lee rail under water, wet bunks, hard tack, bully beef, wish you were here—instead of me!"

John Hancock (1737–93), **patriot and signer of the Declaration of Independence:**
"I shall look forward to a pleasant time."

Hannibal (247–183 B.C.), **Carthaginian general. Poisoning himself in exile:**
"Let me free the Roman people from their long anxiety, since they think it tedious to wait for an old man's death . . . they have sent an ambassador to suggest to Prusias (king of Bithynia) the crime of murdering a guest."

John Wesley Hardin (d. 1895), **outlaw. Shot playing dice:**
"Four sixes to beat!"

Frank Harris (1856–1931), **British writer and *bon viveur*. To his wife:**
"Nellie, my Nellie—I'm going!"

Joel Chandler Harris (1848–1908), **creator of the "Uncle Remus" stories. Asked whether he was feeling better:**
"I am about the extent of a tenth of a gnat's eyebrow better."

Franz Joseph Haydn (1732–1809), **composer:**
"Cheer up, children, I'm all right."

William Hazlitt (1778–1830), **English essayist:**
"Well, I've had a happy life."

Neville Heath (d. 1946), **murderer. Asking for a final whisky:**
"Ah . . . you might make that a double."

Georg Wilhelm Hegel (1770–1831), German philosopher:
"Only one man ever understood me. And he didn't understand me."

Heinrich Heine (1797–1856), German poet. Asked if he was at peace with God:
"Do not trouble yourself. God will pardon me: it's His profession."

Héloise (d. 1164), lover of Abelard:
"In death at last let me rest with Abelard."

Henry IV (1553–1610), King of France. Stabbed in the heart by a religious fanatic called Ravaillac:
"It is nothing."

Henry VIII (1491–1547), King of England:
"Monks! Monks! Monks!"

O. Henry (*nom de plume* of William Sydney Porter) (1862–1910), American writer:
"Turn up the lights; I don't want to go home in the dark."

George Herbert (1593–1638), English poet:
"Lord, forsake me not, now my strength faileth me; but grant me mercy for the merits of my Jesus. And now Lord—Lord now receive my soul."

Myron T. Herrick (1854–1929), American diplomat. Informed by his doctors that he would be "all right":
"Do you really think so? Well, I will do my best."

Abram S. Hewitt (1822–1903), industrialist. Removing his oxygen tube from his mouth:
"And now I am officially dead."

"Wild Bill" Hickok (1837–76), Western folk hero:
"Agnes, darling, if such should be we never meet again, while firing my last shot I will gently breathe the name of my wife—Agnes—and with wishes even for my enemies, I will make the plunge and try to swim to the other shore."

Heinrich Himmler (1900–45), Nazi leader:
"I am Heinrich Himmler."

Thomas Hobbes (1588–1679), English philosopher:
"I am about to take my last long voyage, a great leap in the dark."

Charles Hodge (1797–1878), theologian:
"My work is done. The pins of the tabernacle are taken out."

Hermann Hoeffle (d. 1945), Nazi general:
"Dear Germany."

Hokusai (1760–1849), Japanese painter:
"If Heaven would give me five more years of life, I might become a truly great painter."
"There will be freedom, noble freedom, when one walks abroad in the fields of spring, the soul alone, untrammeled by the body."

Henry Richard Fox Holland (1773–1840), baron, English politician. Of George Selwyn, noted for his interest in corpses and executions:
"If Mr. Selwyn calls again, show him up; if I am alive I shall be delighted to see him, and if I am dead, he would like to see me."

Doc Holliday (d. 1885), gambler and gunfighter. To the person trying to remove his boots:
"Dammit! Put them back on. This is funny."

Oliver Wendell Holmes (1841–1935), Supreme Court Justice. Before he went under the oxygen tent for the last time:
"Lot of damn foolery."

Richard Hooker (1554–1600), English theologian:
"My days are past as a shadow that returns not."

Gerard Manley Hopkins (1844–89), English poet:
"I am so happy, so happy."

Harry Houdini (alias of Erich Weiss) (1874–1926), escapologist:
"I am tired of fighting, Dash (his brother). I guess this thing is going to get me."

A. E. Housman (1859–1936), English scholar and poet. Hearing a joke as he lay on his deathbed:
"I'll tell that story on the golden floor."

Chris Hubbock (d. 1970), newscaster. Shooting herself on a prime time news program:
"And now, in keeping with Channel 40's policy of always bringing you the latest in blood and guts, in living color, you're about to see another first—an attempted suicide."

Victor Hugo (1802–85), French author and dramatist:
"Goodbye, Jeanne, goodbye."

Isaac Hull (1773–1843), admiral:
"I strike my flag."

Henrik Ibsen (1828–1906), Norwegian dramatist. In answer to his wife who said he was looking better:
"On the contrary."

Washington Irving (1783–1859). To his niece:
"Well, I must arrange my pillows for another night. When will this end?"

Thomas Jonathan Jackson (Stonewall Jackson) (1824–63):
"Let us cross over the river and sit under the shade of the trees."

Henry James (1843–1916), writer:
"So here it is at last, the distinguished thing."

Jesse James (1847–82), outlaw and train robber. Trying to remain under cover:
"If anybody passes they'll see me."

William James (1842–1910), philosopher, brother of Henry James:
"It's so good to get home!"

James V (1512–42), King of Scotland:
"The Devil do with it! It will end as it began, it came with a lass and it will go with a lass."

Jeanne d'Arc (1411–31), French heroine and saint. At the stake:
"Oh! My God, go back, father; and when the flame rises round me, lift up the cross that I may see it as I die and speak holy words to me to the last."
"Oh Rouen! I fear you will one day rue my death."
"Water! Water!"

Thomas Jefferson (1743–1826), 3rd U.S. President:
"I resign my soul to God and my daughter to my country."

George Jeffreys (1648–89), **English judge, who presided over the "Bloody Assizes" of 1685:**
"People call me a murderer for doing what at the time was applauded by some who are now high in public favour. They call me a drunkard because I take punch to relieve me in my agony."

Jesus Christ (d. *c.* 33 A.D.). **The Scriptures offer several alternatives:**
"Father, forgive them; for they know not what they do."
"Today shalt thou be with me in Paradise."
"My God, my God, why hast thou forsaken me?"
"Father, into thy hands, I commend my spirit."
"It is finished."

Samuel Johnson (1709–84), **English critic and lexicographer. Hearing that there was no hope of his recovering:**
"Then I will take no more physic, not even my opiates; for I have prayed that I may render up my soul to God unclouded."
"Attend, Francis, to the salvation of your soul, which is the object of greatest importance."
"God bless you, my dear."

Al Jolson (1886–1950), **singer and actor:**
"This is it. I'm going, I'm going."

John Luther Jones (**Casey Jones**) (1864–1900), **railroad locomotive engineer:**
"For I'm going to run her till she leaves the rail—or make it on time with the southbound mail."

Joseph II (1741–90), **Emperor of Germany**:
   "Let my epitaph be: Here lies Joseph, who was unsuccessful in all his undertakings."

Marie Rose Josephine (1763–1814), **Empress of France**:
   "Napoleon! . . . Elba . . . Marie Louise!"

James Joyce (1882–1941), **Irish novelist**:
   "Does anybody understand?"

Judas Iscariot (d. *c.* 33 A.D.):
   "I have sinned in that I have betrayed the innocent blood."

Julian the Apostate (**Flavius Claudius Julianus**) (331–363),
Emperor of Rome:
   "You have conquered, Galilean."

Franz Kafka (1883–1924), **Austrian novelist. He asked Max
Brod to destroy all his work**:
   "There will be no proof that ever I was a writer."

Immanuel Kant (1724–1804), **philosopher**:
   "It is enough."

Terry Kath (d. 1978), **rock musician. Playing Russian roulette with a loaded revolver**:
   "Don't worry it's not loaded."

George S. Kaufman (1889–1961), **playwright**:
   "I'm not afraid any more."

Edmund Kean (1789–1833), **English actor**:
   "Give me another horse . . . Howard!"

John Keats (1795–1821), **English poet:**
"I feel daisies growing over me."
"Severn, lift me up—I am dying—I shall die easy; don't be frightened—be firm and thank God it has come."

Ned Kelly (1855–80), **Australian horse thief and outlaw. On being hanged:**
"Such is life."

"Black Jack" Ketchum (d. 1901), **bank robber and killer. On being hanged:**
"I'll be in hell before you're finished breakfast, boys . . . Let her rip!"

Abdur Rahman Khan (d. 1901), **Emir of Afghanistan:**
"My spirit will remain in Afghanistan, though my soul shall go to God. My last words to you, my son and successor, are never trust the Russians."

William Kidd (1645–1701), **English pirate. After being promised a pardon, he was hanged:**
"This is a very fickle and faithless generation."

"Cholly Knickerbocker" (Maury Paul) (d. 1942), **New York gossip columnist:**
"Oh, Mother, how beautiful it is."

John Knox (1505–72), **Protestant reformer. Asked if he could hear the prayers of friends:**
"Would God that you and all men heard them as I have heard them. I praise God for the heavenly sound.
"Now it is come."

Ronald Knox (1888–1957), English theologian and essayist. Asked if he would like to hear an extract from his own version of the Bible, he declined:

"Awfully jolly of you to suggest it though."

Jimmy Lee Laine, jazz pianist. Dying while playing the piano:

"Let it roll! Let it roll!"

Charles Lamb (1775–1834), English essayist:

"My bedfellows are cramp and cough—we three all in one bed."

Pierre Simon Marquis de Laplace (1749–1827), French scientist:

"What we know is not much; what we do not know is immense."

Hugh Latimer (1485–1555), Bishop of Worcester and Protestant martyr. As he and Nicholas Ridley were being burned in Oxford for heresy:

"Be of good comfort, Master Ridley, and play the man; we shall this day light such a candle, by God's grace, in England, as I trust shall never be put out."

Jean Launes (1769–1815), French Marshal. In answer to Napoleon's comment, "You will live, my friend," he replied:

"I trust I may, if I can still be of use to France and your Majesty."

D. H. Lawrence (1885–1930), English novelist:

"I think it's time for the morphine."

Gertrude Lawrence (1898–1952), British actress. Referring to "The King and I":
"See that Yul (Brynner) gets star billing. He has earned it."

Saint Lawrence (d. 258 A.D.). Roasted alive during persecution by Valerian:
"This side is roasted enough, turn up, oh tyrant great, assay whether roasted or raw thou thinkest the better meat."

Robert E. Lee (1807–70), Confederate commander:
"Strike my tent!"

Franz Lehár (1870–1948), Hungarian composer:
"Now I have finished with all earthly business, and high time too. Yes, yes, my dear child, now comes death."

Leonardo da Vinci (1452–1519):
"I have offended God and mankind because my work didn't reach the quality it should have."

Leopold II (1835–1909), King of Belgium:
"I am hot."

Julie de Lespinasse (1732–76), French society hostess:
"Am I still alive?"

Sinclair Lewis (1885–1951), novelist:
"I am happy. God bless you all."

Franz Liszt (1811–86), Hungarian composer:
"Tristan!"

Richard A. Loeb (d. 1936), murderer. Killed in a prison fight with another inmate, Loeb was slashed with a razor 56 times:

"I think I'm going to make it . . ."

Henry Wadsworth Longfellow (1807–82), American poet. To his sister:

"Now I know that I must be very ill, since you have been sent for."

Louis XIV (1638–1715), King of France:

"Gentlemen, I die in the faith and obedience of the Church. I have followed the advice that I received and have done only what I was desired to do. If I have erred, my guides alone must answer before God, whom I call upon to witness this assertion."

"Oh, my God, come to my aid and hasten to help me."

Louis XVI (1754–93), King of France. From the scaffold:

"Frenchmen, I die innocent: it is from the scaffold and near appearing before God that I tell you so. I pardon my enemies: I desire that France . . ."

Amy Lowell (1874–1925), poet:

"Pete, a stroke . . . Get Eastman!"

Henry Luce (1898–1967), magazine publisher:

"Oh Jesus!"

Martin Luther (1483–1546), founder of Protestantism. Asked if he still held his beliefs:

"Yes."

Niccolò Machiavelli (1469–1527), Italian statesman:
"I desire to go to hell and not to heaven. In the former place I shall enjoy the company of Popes, Kings and Princes, while in the latter are only beggars, monks and apostles."

Cyrus Hall McCormick (1809–84), inventor of the mechanical reaper:
"It's all right, it's all right. I only want heaven."

O. O. McIntyre (d. 1938), newspaper columnist. To his wife:
"Snooks, will you please turn this way. I like to look at your face."

William McKinley (1843–1901), 24th U.S. President. On being assassinated:
"We are all going, we are all going, we are all going . . . oh dear!"

Maurice Maeterlinck (1862–1949), Belgian poet. To his wife:
"For me this is quite natural. It is for you that I am concerned."

Gustav Mahler (1860–1911):
"Mozart."

Malcolm X (Malcolm Little) (d. 1966), Black Muslim leader. Just before he was killed:
"Let's cool it, brothers . . ."

Manuel Laureno Rodriguez "Manolete" (1917–47), matador. Fatally gored by a bull:
"I can't feel anything in my right leg! I can't feel anything in my left leg! Doctor are my eyes open? I can't see!"

Mao Tse-Tung (1893–1976), Chinese leader. There are two versions of his final words:

"Act according to the principles laid down."

"Act in accordance with past principles."

Maria Theresa (1638–83), Queen Consort of France. Replying to a comment on the rain outside:

"Yes, it is indeed frightful weather for a journey as long as the one before me."

Maria Theresa of Austria (1717–80). Asked whether she would like to sleep:

"No, I could sleep, but I must not; death is too near; he must not steal up on me. These fifteen years I have been making ready for him; I will meet him awake."

John Churchill, Duke of Marlborough (1650–1722), English general. Asked if he could hear the prayers that were being said:

"Yes! and I joined in them."

John Marsh (d. 1868), pioneer. To the Mexican bandits who killed him:

"Do you want to kill me?"

Karl Marx (1818–83), political theorist, founder of modern international Communism. To his housekeeper who asked whether he had a final message for the world:

"Go on, get out! Last words are for fools who haven't said enough."

Mary Queen of Scots (1542–87). To Andrew Melville:

"Thou knowest that this world is only vanity and full of trouble and misery. Bear these tidings that I die firm in my religion, a true Catholic, a true Scotch woman, a true French woman. May God forgive those who have sought my death."

"My Lords if you wish to pray for me, I thank you for it, but I cannot join in your prayers, because we are not of the same religion."

"My God, I have hoped in Thee; I commit myself to Thy hands."

Charles Mathews (1776–1835), English comic:
"I am ready."

W. Somerset Maugham (1874–1965), British writer:
"Dying is a very dull, dreary affair. And my advice to you is to have nothing whatever to do with it."

Maximilian (1832–67), Emperor of Mexico. Before the firing squad:
"I die in a just cause. I forgive all, and pray that all may forgive me. May my blood flow for the good of this land. Long live Mexico! . . . Men!"

Lorenzo de Medici (1449–92), ruler of Florence. Asked how he was enjoying his food:
"As a dying man always does."

Baba Meher (d. 1969), guru. His last words were actually spoken in 1925; he lived in silence for the next 44 years:
"Don't worry, be happy."

Felix Mendelssohn (1809–47), composer. Asked how he was feeling:
"Tired, very tired."

Alice Meynell (1847–1922), English poet and essayist:
"This is not tragic. I am happy."

Michelangelo di Lodovico Buonarroti (1475–1564), Italian painter and sculptor:
"My soul I resign to God, my body to the earth, and my worldly possessions to my relations."

Draza Mihajlovic (1893–1946), Serbian guerrilla. Before facing the firing squad:
"I found myself in a whirl of events and intrigues. I found Destiny was merciless towards me when it threw me into the most difficult whirlwinds. I wanted much, I began much, but the whirlwind, the world whirlwind, carried me and my work away."

John Stuart Mill (1806–73), philosopher. On being told that he would never recover:
"My work is done."

John Milton (1608–74), poet. To his wife:
"Make much of me as long as I live, for thou knowest I have given thee all when I die at thy disposal."

Wilson Mizner (d. 1933), Hollywood impresario. To his doctor:
"Well, Doc, I guess this is the main event!"
To an attendant priest:
"Why should I talk to you? I've just been talking to your boss."

Mohammed (570–632), prophet:
"Oh Allah, be it so."

Molière (Jean Baptiste Poquelin) (1622–73), French play-wright:
"There is no need to be frightened. You have seen me spit more blood than that and to spare. Nevertheless, go and ask my wife to come up to me."

James, Duke of Monmouth (1649–85). To the executioner:
"Prithee, let me feel the axe . . . I fear it is not sharp enough."

Lady Mary Wortley Montagu (1689–1762), English writer:
"It has all been very interesting."

Dwight Lyman Moody (1837–99), evangelist:
"Earth recedes, heaven opens. I've been through the gates! Don't call me back . . . if this is death, it's sweet. Dwight! Irene! I see the children's faces."
(Dwight and Irene were his dead grandchildren)

Sir John Moore (1761–1809), British soldier. To the surgeon:
"You can be of no service to me, go to the soldiers, to whom you can be useful.
"I hope the people of England will be satisfied and that my country will do me justice."

Thomas B. Moran (d. 1971), American pickpocket:
"I've never forgiven that smartalecky reporter who named me 'butterfingers'—to me it's not funny."

Hannah More (1745–1833), English poet:
"Joy!"

Saint Thomas More (1478–1535), English statesman. **To the executioner:**
"Pluck up thy spirits, man, and be not afraid to do thy office."
Moving his beard from the reach of the axe:
"Pity that should be cut that has never committed treason."

Modest Moussorgsky (1835–81), Russian composer:
"It is the end. Woe is me!"

Wolfgang Amadeus Mozart (1756–91). **Referring to the score of the Requiem Mass on which he was working:**
"Did I not tell you that I was writing this for myself?"

Benito Mussolini (1883–1945), Italian dictator. **To the partisan who shot him:**
"But . . . but . . . Colonel . . ."

Viscount Horatio Nelson (1758–1805), British admiral:
"God bless you, Hardy."
"Thank God, I have done my duty."
"God and my country."

Nero (37–68), **Emperor of Rome:**
"What an artist perishes in me!"
Quoting Homer:
"The galloping of speedy steeds assails my frighted ears."

Sir Isaac Newton (1642–1727), English philosopher and physicist:
"I do not know what I seem to the world, but to myself I appear to have been like a boy playing upon the seashore and diverting myself by now and then finding a smoother

pebble or prettier shell than ordinary, while the great ocean of truth lay before me all undiscovered."

Sir William Robert Nicoll (1851–1923), **minister and theologian:**
"I believe everything that I have written about immortality."

Vaslav Nijinsky (1890–1950), **ballet dancer:**
"Mamasha!"

John Noyes (d. 1555), **Protestant martyr. Burnt at the stake:**
"We shall not lose our lives in this fire, but change them for a better. And for coals have pearls."

Lawrence E. G. Oates (1880–1912), **member of Scott's fated expedition to the South Pole. Believing that he was a burden to his companions he left the tent during a blizzard saying:**
"I am just going outside and may be some time."

Titus Oates (1649–1705), **English conspirator, creator of the "Popish Plot":**
"It is all the same in the end."

Torlogh O'Carolan (d. 1838), **Irish poet. Asking for his final whiskey:**
"It would be hard if such friends should part at least without kissing."

Wilfred Owen (1893–1918), **English poet. To one of his men, just before he was killed in World War I action:**
"Well done . . . You are doing very well, my boy."

Thomas Paine (1737–1809), radical political theorist, born in England, died in America:

His doctor: "Your belly diminishes."

Paine: "And yours augments."

William Palmer (1824–56). Hanged for poisoning a friend. Stepping onto the gallows trap:

"Are you sure it's safe?"

Viscount Henry John Temple Palmerston (1784–1865), English statesman:

"Die, my dear doctor? That's the last thing I shall do."

Carl Panzram (1891–1930). Executed after being convicted of murdering 23 people:

"I wish the human race had one neck and I had my hands round it."

Gram Parsons (d. 1972), rock musician. Told that his drug abuse would kill him:

"Death is a warm cloak and old friend. I regard death as something that comes up on a roulette wheel every once in a while."

Blaise Pascal (1623–62), French mathematician and theologian:

"Forsake me not, O my God."

Boris Pasternak (1890–1960), Russian novelist:

"Goodbye . . . why am I hemorrhaging?"

Louis Pasteur (1822–95), scientist. Offered a glass of milk:

"I cannot."

Anna Pavlova (1885–1931), prima ballerina:
"Get my *Swan* costume ready!"

Charles Peace (1832–79), English murderer:
"What is the scaffold? A short cut to heaven."

Charles Willson Peale (1741–1827), American painter:
Peale: "Sybilla, feel my pulse."
Daughter: "I can't feel any."
Peale: "I thought not."

Charles Péguy (1873–1914), French writer:
"Keep firing."

Boies Penrose (1860–1921), Senator from Pennsylvania. To his valet:
"See here, William. See here. I don't want any of your damned lies. How do I look? Am I getting any better? The truth now . . . All right, William. When you go to church tomorrow—pray for me, too."

Spencer Perceval (1762–1812), British statesman. Assassinated while Prime Minister:
"Murder!"

Pericles (490–429 B.C.), Athenian statesman:
"No Athenian, through my means, ever wore mourning."

Count Pestel (d. 1826), Russian revolutionary. The rope broke on the first attempt to hang him:
"Stupid country, where they do not even know how to hang."

St. John Philby (d. 1960), Arabic scholar:
   "God, I'm bored."

David Graham Phillips (1867–1911), novelist:
   "I could have one against two bullets but not against six."

Pablo Picasso (1881–1973), painter:
   "Drink to me."

Luigi Pirandello (1867–1936), Italian dramatist:
   "The hearse, the horse, the driver, and—enough!"

William Pitt, the Younger (1759–1806), English Prime Minister:
   "My country! How I love my country!"
   "I could do with one of Bellamy's veal pies."

Orville H. Platt (1827–1905), U.S. Senator:
   "You know what this means, Doctor, and so do I."

Plotinus (205–270), Roman philosopher:
   "I am making my last effort to return that which is divine in me to that which is divine in the universe."

Edgar Allan Poe (1809–49), American writer:
   "Lord help my poor soul."

James Knox Polk (1795–1849), 11th U.S. President. To his wife:
   "I love you Sarah—I—love—you."

Madame de Pompadour (1688–1744), French courtesan. To the priest who was about to leave:

"One moment, Monsieur le Curé, and we will depart together."

Alexander Pope (1688–1744), English poet:

"There is nothing meritorious but virtue and friendship, and indeed friendship itself is only a part of virtue."

When asked if a priest should be called to him:

"I do not think it essential, but it will be very right, and I thank you for putting me in mind of it."

Joseph Priestley (1733–1804), English chemist. After finishing a few corrections and alterations in his work:

"That is right: I have now done."

Marcel Proust (1871–1922), French novelist. Asked by his brother if he was hurting him:

"Yes, Robert dear, you are."

Alexander Pushkin (1799–1837), Russian poet. Gazing at his books:

"Farewell, my friends."

François Rabelais (1490–1553), French writer:

"I go to seek the great Perhaps."

Sir Walter Raleigh (1552–1618), English courtier and explorer. To a friend unable to approach the scaffold:

"I know not how it may be with you, but I shall be sure to find a place."

Of the axe:
" 'Tis a sharp medicine, but a sound cure for all diseases."
"It matters not how the head lies, provided the heart be right."
"Now I am going to God."
To the executioner:
"What dost thou fear? Strike, man!"

Sanzio Raphael (1483–1520), Italian painter:
"Happy."

Maurice Ravel (1875–1937), French composer. Seeing his bandaged head in the mirror:
"I look like a Moor."

Madame Jeanne Récamier (1777–1849), celebrated French society beauty:
"We shall meet again."

Frederic Remington (1861–1909), American painter. Informed that he would have to undergo an appendectomy:
"Cut her loose, Doc!"

Pierre Auguste Renoir (1841–1919), French painter:
"I am still progressing."

Sir Joshua Reynolds (1723–92), English painter:
"I know that all things on earth must have an end and I have come to mine."

Cecil Rhodes (1853–1902), British Empire builder:
"So little done, so much to do."

Cardinal Armand Richelieu (1585–1642). As the Viaticum was being prepared for him:

"Here is my judge by whom I shall be judged; and I sincerely implore Him to pronounce my condemnation if I have ever had any other intention save the welfare of religion and of the state."

Rittmeister Manfred Freiherr von Richthofen ("The Red Baron") (1882–1918), German fighter pilot. To his mechanics:

"Don't you think I'll be back."

Nicholas Ridley (1500–55), Protestant martyr. Burned for heresy in Oxford, with Hugh Latimer:

"Let the fire come unto me, I cannot burn. Lord, have mercy upon me."

James W. Rodgers (1911–60), murderer executed by a firing squad in Utah. Asked whether he had a final request:

"Why, yes—a bullet-proof vest."

Erwin Rommel (1891–1944), German Field-Marshal. Ordered to commit suicide by Hitler, he explained it to his son:

"To die by the hand of one's own people is hard."

Franklin D. Roosevelt (1882–1945), 31st U.S. President:

"I have a terrific headache."

Theodore Roosevelt (1858–1919), 25th U.S. President. To his servant:

"Please put out the light."

Robbie Ross (d. 1918), friend of Oscar Wilde. Punning on Keats's epitaph:

"Here lies one whose name was written in hot water."

Nathan Meyer Rothschild (1777–1836) of the European family of financiers:

"Poor unhappy me! A victim to nervousness and fancied terrors! And all because of my money."

Jean Jacques Rousseau (1712–78), French political theorist:

"See the sun, whose smiling face calls me, see that immeasurable light. There is God! Yes, God himself, who is opening His arms and inviting me to taste at last that eternal and unchanging joy that I had so long desired."

Rob Roy (Robert MacGregor) (1671–1734), clan leader during the Jacobite rebellion in Scotland:

"Now all is over—let the piper play 'We Return No More'."

Nikolai Rubinstein (1835–81), founder of the Moscow Conservatoire and brother of the pianist Anton:

"Oysters! Nothing will do me as much good as a dozen cold oysters and an ice afterwards."

Damon Runyon (1884–1946), American author and journalist:

"You can keep the things of bronze and stone and give me one man to remember me just once a year."

Sadi (1184?–1291), Persian poet:

"Better is the sinner who hath thoughts about God, than the saint who hath only the show of sanctity."

Augustus Saint-Gaudens (1848–1907), Irish-American sculptor. Gazing at the sunset:

"It's very beautiful, but I want to go farther away."

Samson (1161–1120 B.C.):

"O Lord God, remember me, I pray thee and strengthen me, only this once, O God, that I may be at once avenged of the Philistines for my two eyes."

"Let me die with the Philistines."

Maurice de Saxe (1696–1750), French soldier:

"The dream has been short; but it has been fine."

Friedrich von Schiller (1759–1805), German poet and dramatist. Asked how he felt:

"Calmer and calmer."

Franz Schubert (1797–1828), German composer. On being told he was in his own bed:

"No! It is not true; Beethoven is not laid here."

"Here, here is my end."

"Dutch" Schultz (d. 1935), American gangster:

"Turn your back to me, please Henry, I am so sick now. The police are getting many complaints. Look out for Jimmy Valentine, for he's a friend of mine. Come on, come on, Jim. OK, OK, I am all through. I can't do another thing. Look out mamma, Helen, please take me out. I will settle the incident. Come on open the soak duckets; the chimney sweeps. Talk to the sword. Shut up, you big mouth! Please help me to get up. Henry! Max! Come over here. French Canadian bean soup. I want to pay. Let them leave me alone."

Moritz von Schwind (1804–71), Austrian painter. Asked how he felt:

"Excellent."

Edward "Death Valley Scotty" Scott (d. 1954), American recluse:

"I got four things to live by: don't say nothin' that will hurt anybody; don't give advice—nobody will take it anyway; don't complain; don't explain."

Robert Falcon Scott (1868–1912), British explorer. He and his comrades perished on their return trek from the South Pole. The search party found this diary:

"We are showing that Englishmen can still die with a bold spirit, fighting it out to the end . . . Had we lived, I should have had a tale to tell of the hardihood, endurance and courage of companions which would have stirred the heart of every Englishman. These rough notes and our dead bodies must tell the tale . . . It seems a pity but I do not think I can write more."

Winfield Scott (1786–1866), American general:

"Peter, take good care of my horse."

Edward Wyllis Scripps (1854–1926), American newspaper publisher:

"Too many cigars this evening, I guess."

John Sedgwick (1813–64), American Civil War general. Carelessly peering over the parapet at the battle of Spotsylvania:

"They couldn't hit an elephant at this dist . . ."

Sir Henry Segrave (1896–1930), British racing driver. Killed while attempting to break the world water speed record:
"Did we do it?"

Lucius Seneca (3 B.C.–65 A.D.), Roman poet. After entering a pool of water he sprinkled some on the bystanders, saying:
"A libation to Jupiter the liberator."

Marie de Sévigné (1626–96), French writer and court lady. Criticizing her supposed vanity, the priest said:
"Remember, all your beauty will turn to dust and ashes."
To which she replied:
"Yes, but I'm not yet dust and ashes!"

Sir Ernest Henry Shackleton (1874–1922), explorer. To his doctor:
"You are always wanting me to give up something. What do you want me to give up now?"

George Bernard Shaw (1856–1950), Irish dramatist. To his nurse:
"Sister, you're trying to keep me alive as an old curiosity. But I'm done, I'm finished. I'm going to die."

Richard Brinsley Sheridan (1751–1816), English dramatist:
"I am absolutely undone and broken-hearted."

Algernon Sidney (1622?–1683), conspirator against King Charles II. Asked by the executioner, "Will you rise again?":
"Not until the general resurrection."

Sir Philip Sidney (1554–86), English scholar, soldier, and statesman. Giving his water-bottle to a fellow wounded soldier:

"Thy necessity is greater than mine."

"I do humbly intreat the Lord with trembling heart that the pangs of death may not be so grievous as to take away my understanding."

"I would not change my joy for the empire of the world."

Adam Smith (1723–90), English political economist:

"I believe that we must adjourn the meeting to some other place."

Captain E. J. Smith (d. 1912), master of the *S.S. Titanic:*

"Let me go."

Joseph Smith (1805–44), founder of the Mormon church. Killed by a mob:

"That's right, brother Taylor, parry them off as well as you can."

Socrates (469–430 B.C.), Greek philosopher. Taking poison, he said:

"Crito, I owe a cock to Aesculapius; do not forget to pay it."

Sir Stanley Spencer (1891–1959), English painter. To the nurse who had just given him an injection:

"Beautifully done."

Stanislas I (1677–1766), King of Poland. Referring to the bathrobe which caught fire, causing the burns from which he died:

"You gave it to me to warm me, but it has kept me too hot."

Konstantin Stanislavsky (1863–1938), Director of the Moscow Art Theatre. Asked if he wanted to send a message to his sister in a letter which was being written to her:
"I've lots to say to her, not just something. But not now. I'm sure to get it all mixed up."

Sir Henry Morton Stanley (1841–1904), explorer:
"Four o'clock. How strange. So that is the time. Strange. Enough!"

Laurence Sterne (1713–68), English novelist:
"Now, it has come."

Robert Louis Stevenson (1850–94), novelist:
"My head, my head!"

Lucy Stone (1818–93), American suffragette:
"Make the world better."

Lytton Strachey (1880–1938), English biographer and critic:
"If this is dying, I don't think much of it."

Johann Strauss (1825–99), Austrian composer. When advised to go to sleep:
"I will whatever happens."

August Strindberg (1849–1912), Swedish dramatist. Clasping a Bible:
"Everything is atoned for."

Sun Yat-sen (1866–1925), liberator of China:
"Peace, struggle, save China."

Jonathan Swift (1667–1745), **British satirist:**
"I am dying like a poisoned rat in a hole. I am what I am!
I am what I am!"

Carl Alfalfa Switzer (1926–59), **child star of "Our Gang"
films who ended his life as a drunk, killed by another drunk:**
"I want that fifty bucks you owe me and I want it now."

General Penn Symons (d. 1899), **British soldier. Killed in
action during the Boer War:**
"I am severely—mortally—wounded in the stomach."

John Millington Synge (1871–1909), **Irish dramatist:**
"It's no use fighting death any longer."

Robert A. Taft (1889–1953), **U.S. Senator. To his wife:**
"Well, Martha . . . ! Glad to see you looking so well."

Tamburlaine (1336–1405), **Mongol leader:**
"Never has death been frightened away by screaming."

Bayard Taylor (1825–78), **American writer and traveller:**
"I want—I want, oh, you know what I mean, that stuff of
life!"

Zachary Taylor (1784–1850), **12th U.S. President:**
"I am about to die, I expect the summons soon. I have en-
deavored to discharge all my official duties faithfully. I re-
gret nothing, but am sorry that I am about to leave my
friends."

Dylan Thomas (1914–53), **Welsh poet:**
"I've had eighteen straight whiskies. I think that's the
record."

Told later that his nightmare delirium tremens would go away, he answered:
"Yes, I believe you."

"Big Bill" Thompson (d. 1944), mayor of Chicago:
"Everything is all set, Jim . . . that's right, that's right."

Henry David Thoreau (1817–62), American naturalist and writer:
"Moose . . . Indian . . ."

James Thurber (1894–1961), American writer:
"God bless . . . God damn . . ."

Hideki Tojo (1885–1948), Japanese politician and soldier:
"Oh, look, see how the cherry blossoms fall mutely."

Leo Tolstoy (1828–1910), Russian novelist. To his daughter, Alexandra:
"Come closer—it is so simple . . . to seek, always to seek."
Later, to his son Sergei:
"To escape . . . I must escape . . . ! Truth . . . I love much."

Sir Herbert Beerbohm Tree (1851–1917), English actor. Thinking of his forthcoming role:
"I shall not need to study the part at all. I know it already."

Leon Trotsky (1879–1940), Russian revolutionary leader. On his way to hospital:
"I feel here that this time they have succeeded."

Vicomte de Turenne (1611–75), French soldier. Dying at the battle of Salzbach:
"I did not mean to be killed today."

J. M. W. Turner (1775–1851), English painter:
"The sun is God."

Mark Twain (*nom de plume* of Samuel Langhorne Clemens) (1835–1910), American humorist. To his daughter:
"Goodbye . . . If we meet . . ."

John Tyler (1790–1862), 10th U.S. President:
"I am going . . . perhaps it is for the best."

William Tyndale (1491–1536), English translator of the Bible. At the stake:
"Lord, open the King of England's eyes."

John Tyndall (1820–93), British physicist. After being accidentally given an overdose of chloral by his wife:
"Yes, my poor darling, you have killed your John! . . . Let us do all we can. Tickle my throat. Get a stomach pump . . . Yes, I know you are all trying to rouse me."

Tzu-Hsi (1834–1908), Empress dowager of China:
"Never again allow a woman to hold the supreme power in the State. It is against the house-law of our dynasty and should be forbidden. Be careful not to allow eunuchs to meddle in government matters. The Ming dynasty was brought to ruin by eunuchs, and its fate should be a warning to my people."

Wilbur Underhill (d. 1934), American bank robber. Shot by police:

"Tell the boys I'm coming home."

Rudolph Valentino (1895–1926), movie idol:

"Don't pull down the blinds! I feel fine. I want the sunlight to greet me."

William Henry Vanderbilt (1821–85), American financier:

"The care of 200 millions of dollars is too great a load for any brain or back to bear. It is enough to kill a man. There is no pleasure to be got out of it as an offset—no good of any kind. I have no real gratification of enjoyment of any sort more than my neighbor on the next block who is worth only half a million."

Paul Verlaine (1844–96), French poet. In answer to a friend who whispered "He's dying":

"Don't sole the dead man's shoes yet."

Vespasian (9–79), Roman emperor:

"An emperor ought to die standing. I think I am now becoming a God."

Victor Emmanuel II (1820–78), King of Italy. When told that he would never recover:

"Is it come to that? Then send for the priest."

Victoria (1819–1901), Queen of England:

"Bertie."

François Marie Arouet de Voltaire (1694–1778), **French man of letters. Asked if he recognized the divinity of Christ:**
"In the name of God, let me die in peace!"

Richard Wagner (1813–83), **German composer:**
"I am fond of them, of the inferior beings of the abyss, of those who are full of longing."

Karl Wallenda (d. 1978), **high-wire performer. Killed performing in Puerto Rico:**
"The only place I feel alive is the high wires."

Archbishop Warham (1450–1532), **English prelate. Informed that he still had some $60.00 in cash:**
"That is enough to last until I get to heaven."

George Washington (1732–99). **To Dr. Craik:**
"Doctor, I die hard, but I am not afraid to go."
To Dr. Brown:
"I feel myself going. I thank you for your attention; but I pray you to take no more trouble for me. Let me go quietly, as I cannot last long."

Daniel Webster (1782–1852), **American orator, lawyer, statesman:**
"I still live . . . poetry."

Noah Webster (1758–1843), **American lexicographer:**
"I have struggled with many difficulties. Some I have been able to overcome and by some I have been overcome. I have made many mistakes but I love my country and have labored for the youth of my country, and I trust no precept of mine has taught any dear youth to sin."

H. G. Wells (1866–1946), British writer. To his nurse:
"Go away. I'm all right."

John Wesley (1703–91), English evangelist and founder of Methodism:
"The best of all is, God is with us."
"I'll praise, I'll praise—Farewell."

Walter White (1893–1954), Black leader. Asked how he liked his daughter's style of dress:
"I plead the Fifth Amendment."

Walt Whitman (1819–91), American poet:
"Oh dear, he's a good fellow."

Oscar Wilde (1856–1900), Irish playwright. Calling for champagne:
"I am dying, as I have lived, beyond my means."

William the Silent (1533–84), founder of the Dutch republic. Asked whether he trusted his soul to Jesus Christ:
"Yes."

William III (1650–1701), King of England. To his doctors:
"I know that you have done all that skill and learning could do for me; but the case is beyond your art, and I submit."

Jan de Witt (1625–72), Dutch statesman. To the mob which killed him:
"What are you doing? This is not what you wanted."

James Wolfe (1727–59), British soldier. Hearing the news of his victory at Quebec, over the French:
"Then I die happy."

William Wordsworth (1770–1850), **English poet. Asked whether he wished to receive the sacrament:**
"That is just what I want."
"Is that you, Dora?"

Brigham Young (1801–77), **Mormon leader:**
"Amen."

Eugène Ysaye (1858–1931), **Belgian violinist, listening to his own Fourth Sonata:**
"Splendid, the finale just a little too fast."

Florenz Ziegfeld (1869–1932), **American impresario. He imagined himself once again at the first night of the "Follies":**
"Curtain! Fast music! Light! Ready for the last finale! Great! The show looks good, the show looks good."

John Ziska (1360–1434), **Czech revolutionary leader:**
"Make my skin into drum-heads for the Bohemian cause."

Emile Zola (1840–1902), **French novelist:**
"I feel sick. My head is splitting. No, don't you see the dog is sick too. We are both ill. It must be something we have eaten. It will pass away. Let us not bother them."

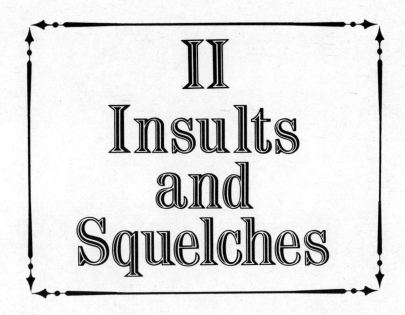

II
Insults
and
Squelches

"You should learn not to make personal remarks," said Alice to the Mad Hatter. Fortunately for us he never learned. Personal remarks aren't polite, aren't pleasant, aren't politic, but they can be such fun!

This chapter is a collection of personal remarks that can fairly claim to be classified as the Last Words of the Living in that when they were first uttered they were fairly unanswerable: they were lines with which to end a conversation—if not a friendship! The hundred or more insults, ripostes and squelches you will find here are lines that it would be hard to follow, even with the advantage of hindsight and the time to sharpen your wit at leisure.

In my view the great mistress of the art of delivering the line that brooks no response was Margot Asquith, the wife of Britain's Liberal Prime Minister at the beginning of the 20th century. Her memorable quips are many:

She described an American general as "an imitation rough diamond."

Of a politician she observed, "He had one arm round your waist and one eye on the clock."

Of Lloyd George, who became British Prime Minister after Asquith in 1916, she said, "He could never see a belt without hitting below it."

Of her husband she commented, "His modesty amounts to deformity."

Of a female acquaintance she said, "She tells enough white lies to ice a cake."

Margot Asquith's American counterpart, of course, was Dorothy Parker. Indeed when Miss Parker reviewed Lady Asquith's long autobiography, she commented: "The affair between Margot Asquith and Margot Asquith will live as one of the prettiest love stories in all literature."

Dorothy Parker certainly said more witty things than most people, but probably not quite as many as are attributed to her. Once you get a reputation for wit, it seems that people are ever anxious to put funny words into your mouth —whether or not they legitimately belong there. I've done my best to give credit where it's due, but because so many of the witticisms of our time are either apocryphal or generated by gagwriters or a well-oiled publicity machine, I've divided the examples into two categories. The first is an A to Z of tart one-liners each one of which I believe actually was spoken or written by the person for whom it is claimed. The second is a series of anecdotes, whose pedigree may well be quite as sound, but which it is rather more difficult to establish.

Joseph Addison (1672–1719), **English essayist passing judgment on the poet John Milton:**
"Our language sunk under him."

Fred Allen (1894–1956), **radio comedian:**
"California is a fine place to live in—if you happen to be an orange."

Benjamin F. Bache (1769–98), **editor of "Aurora":**
"If ever a nation was debauched by a man, the American nation has been debauched by Washington . . . If ever a nation was deceived by a man, the American nation has been deceived by Washington."

James M. Barrie (1860–1937), **novelist and playwright:**
"There are few more impressive sights in the world than a Scotsman on the make."

Sir Thomas Beecham (1878–1961), **British conductor:**
"There are no women composers, never have been, and possibly never will be."

Max Beerbohm (1872–1956), essayist and caricaturist. On the pre-Raphaelite painter William Morris:

"Of course we all know that Morris was a wonderful all-round man, but the act of walking round him has always tired me."

Ludwig van Beethoven (1770–1827), to a fellow composer:

"I liked your opera. I think I will set it to music."

Brendan Behan (1923–64), Irish author:

"Montreal is the only place where a good French accent isn't a social asset."

Aneurin Bevan (1897–1965), British socialist politician, on fellow politician Neville Chamberlain:

"He has the lucidity which is the by-product of a fundamentally sterile mind. . . . Listening to a speech by Chamberlain is like paying a visit to Woolworth's; everything in its place and nothing above sixpence."

Napoleon Bonaparte (1769–1821), on women:

"Nature intended women to be our slaves . . . they are our property; we are not theirs. They belong to us, just as a tree that bears fruit belongs to a gardener. What a mad idea to demand equality for women! . . . Women are nothing but machines for producing children."

William Cowper Brann (1855–98), on President McKinley:

"Why, if a man were to call my dog McKinley, and the brute failed to resent to the death the damning insult, I'd drown it."

John Mason Brown (1900–69), American critic:

"Tallulah Bankhead barged down the Nile last night as Cleopatra—and sank."

Al Capone (1899–1947), Chicago gangster:
"I don't even know what street Canada is on."

Al Capp (b. 1909), cartoonist, on modern painting:
"Abstract art? A product of the untalented, sold by the unprincipled to the utterly bewildered."

Thomas Carlyle (1795–1881), Scottish historian, on Napoleon III:
"His mind was a kind of extinct sulphur-pit."

Lady Violet Bonham Carter (1874–1965), on the British economist and statesman Sir Stafford Cripps:
"Sir Stafford has a brilliant mind—until it is made up."

The Chicago Times **(1863), on the Gettysburg Address:**
". . . We did not conceive it possible that even Mr Lincoln would produce a paper so slipshod, so loose-joined, so puerile, not alone in literary construction, but in its ideas, its sentiments, its grasp. He has outdone himself. He has literally come out of the little end of his own horn. By the side of it, mediocrity is superb."

Sir Winston Churchill (1874–1965), on the socialist politician Clement Attlee:
"A modest little man with much to be modest about."

Henry Clay (1777–1850), on John C. Calhoun:
"A rigid, fanatic, ambitious, selfishly partisan and sectional turncoat with too much genius and too little common sense, who will either die a traitor or a madman."

Georges Clemenceau (1841–1920), French statesman:
"America is the only nation in history which miraculously has gone directly from barbarism to degeneration without the usual interval of civilization."

Sir Noel Coward (1899–1973), on a man of slight stature:
"He's a little man, that's his trouble. Never trust a man with short legs—brains too near their bottoms."

e. e. cummings (1894–1962), on President Warren Harding's death:
"The only man, woman or child who wrote a simple declarative sentence with seven grammatical errors, is dead."

Benjamin Disraeli (1804–81), on fellow politician Lord John Russell, leader of the British Liberals:
"If a traveller were informed that such a man was the Leader of the House of Commons, he might begin to comprehend how the Egyptians worshipped an insect."

Clifton Fadiman (b. 1904), American commentator:
"The German mind has a talent for making no mistakes but the very greatest."

Eugene Field (1850–95), on the performance of Creston Clarke as Shakespeare's King Lear:
"He played the King as though under a momentary apprehension that someone else was about to play the ace."

W. C. Fields (1879–1946), on being asked whether he liked children:
"Boiled or fried?"

A. J. Fifield, editor, sent this rejection slip to authoress Gertrude Stein (1874–1946), parodying her eccentric experimental style:

"I am only one, only one, only one. Only one being, one at the same time. Not two, not three, only one. Only one life to live, only sixty minutes in one hour. Only one pair of eyes. Only one brain. Only one being. Being only one, having only one pair of eyes, having only one time, having only one life, I cannot read your MS three or four times. Not even one time. Only one look, only one look is enough. Hardly one copy would sell here. Hardly one. Hardly one."

Benjamin Franklin (1706–90) sent this letter to William Stahan:

"You and I were long friends; you are now my enemy, and I am

> Yours,
> B. Franklin."

John Nance Garner (1869–1967), U.S. Vice President under Franklin D. Roosevelt:

"The Vice-Presidency ain't worth a pitcher of warm spit."

W. S. Gilbert (1836–1911), on Sir Herbert Beerbohm Tree's portrayal of Hamlet:

"Funny without being vulgar."

Edmond de Goncourt (1822–96), French novelist, on a dinner at a fellow writer's new house:

"House-warming at Zola's . . . very tasty dinner . . . including some grouse whose scented flesh Daudet compared to an old courtesan's flesh marinaded in a bidet."

Margaret Halsey (1938), American writer:
"Englishwomen's shoes look as if they had been made by someone who had often heard shoes described, but had never seen any."

O. Henry (1862–1910), American writer:
"If there ever was an aviary overstocked with jays it is that Yaptown-on-the-Hudson called New York."

Justice Oliver Wendell Holmes (1841–1935):
"You may have genius. The contrary is, of course, probable."

A. E. Housman (1859–1936), British classical scholar and critic, on a fellow poet, Elias Stoeber:
"Stoeber's mind, though that is no name to call it by . . . turns as unswervingly to the false, the meaningless, the unmetrical, as the needle to the pole."

Sam Houston (1793–1863), on Jefferson Davis:
"Yes, I know Mr. Davis. He is as ambitious as Lucifer, cold as a snake, and what he touches will not prosper."

Gordie Howe (1975), hockey star:
"All pro athletes are bilingual. They speak English and profanity."

Paul Hume (1950), music critic of the *Washington Post*, on a recital by singer Margaret Truman:
"Miss Truman is a unique American phenomenon with a pleasant voice of little size and fair quality . . . yet Miss Truman cannot sing very well. She is flat a good deal of the time . . . she communicates almost nothing of the music she presents . . . There are few moments during her recital

when one can relax and feel confident that she will make her goal, which is the end of the song."

Thomas Jefferson (1743–1826), on Plato:
"Take from him his sophisms, futilities and incomprehensibilities and what remains? His foggy mind."

Samuel Johnson (1709–84):
"I am willing to love all mankind, except an American."

Murray Kempton, journalist, on Franklin D. Roosevelt:
"I have always found Roosevelt an amusing fellow, but I would not employ him, except for reasons of personal friendship, as a geek in a common carnival."

John F. Kennedy (1917–63), on John G. Diefenbaker, Canadian Prime Minister:
"I couldn't have called him an s.o.b.—I didn't know he was one—at the time."

Walter Kerr (b. 1913), theatre critic:
"*Hook and Ladder* is the sort of play that gives failures a bad name."

Rudyard Kipling (1865–1936), English writer:
"A woman is only a woman,
But a good cigar is a smoke."

Henry Labouchere (1798–1869), English statesman, on William Gladstone, British Prime Minister:
"I don't object to the Old Man's always having the ace of trumps up his sleeve, but merely to his belief that God Almighty put it there."

D. H. Lawrence (1885–1930), English writer:
"My God, what a clumsy *olla putrida* James Joyce is! Nothing but old fags and cabbage-stumps of quotations from the Bible and the rest, stewed in the juice of deliberate, journalistic dirty-mindedness."

Charles Lee (1731–82), American general, on George Washington:
"That dark designing sordid ambitious vain proud arrogant and vindictive knave."

Abraham Lincoln (1809–65), to his general in the field, George B. McClellan:
"My dear McClellan: if you don't want to use the army I should like to borrow it for a while. Yours respectfully,
                                                            A. Lincoln."

Alice Roosevelt Longworth (b. 1884), daughter of President Theodore Roosevelt, on Calvin Coolidge:
"He looks as if he had been weaned on a pickle."

Thomas B. Macaulay (1800–59), English historian, on Socrates:
"The more I read him, the less I wonder that they poisoned him."

Groucho Marx (1895–1977), American comic actor:
"From the moment I picked your book up until I laid it down I was convulsed with laughter. Some day I intend reading it."

W. Somerset Maugham (1874–1965), British writer:
"American women expect to find in their husbands the perfection that English women only hope to find in their butlers."

H. L. Mencken (1880–1956), American journalist and lexicographer:
"Democracy is a form of religion. It is the worship of jackals by jackasses."

Friedrich Nietzsche (1844–1900), German philosopher:
"Marriage makes an end of many short follies—being one long stupidity."

Dorothy Parker (1893–1967), American wit:
"That woman speaks eighteen languages, and she can't say 'No' in any of them."

Madame de Pompadour (1721–64), greeting the news of the fall of Quebec:
"It makes little difference; Canada is useful only to provide me with furs."

John Randolph (1773–1833), Virginia politician, on Edward Livingstone:
"He was a man of splendid abilities but utterly corrupt. Like rotten mackerel by moonlight, he shines and stinks."

Thomas Reed (1839–1902), Speaker of the House of Representatives, on members of Congress:
"They never open their mouths without subtracting from the sum of human knowledge."

Theodore Roosevelt (1858–1915), while Vice President under McKinley:
   "McKinley has a chocolate-éclair backbone."

Gioacchino Antonio Rossini (1792–1868), Italian composer:
   "Wagner has beautiful moments but awful quarter hours."

John Ruskin (1819–1900), English poet:
   "Beethoven always sounds to me like the upsetting of a bag of nails, with here and there an also-dropped hammer."

Bertrand Russell (1872–1970), English political philosopher:
   "In his youth, Wordsworth sympathized with the French Revolution, went to France, wrote good poetry, and had a natural daughter. At this period, he was a 'bad' man. Then he became 'good,' abandoned his daughter, adopted correct principles, and wrote bad poetry."

Carl Sandburg (1863–1952), American poet:
   "Here is the difference between Dante, Milton, and me. They wrote about hell and never saw the place. I wrote about Chicago after looking the town over for years and years."

George Santayana (1863–1952), American philosopher:
   "Boston is a moral and intellectual nursery always busy applying first principles to trifles."

George Bernard Shaw (1856–1950), on Theodore Roosevelt:
   "His idea of getting hold of the right end of the stick is to snatch it from the hands of somebody who is using it effectively, and hit him over the head with it."

And Shaw, on the United States:

"You are right in your impression that a number of persons are urging me to come to the United States. But why on earth do you call them my friends?"

General Philip H. Sheridan (1831–88):

"If I owned Texas and Hell, I would rent out Texas and live in Hell."

Louis Sherwin, American writer, on Hollywood:

"They know only one word of more than one syllable here, and that is fillum."

Sydney Smith (1771–1845), British clergyman, journalist and wit:

"I like him and his wife. He is so ladylike, and she is such a perfect gentleman."

Duncan Spaeth, American writer and academic:

"I know why the sun never sets on the British Empire: God wouldn't trust an Englishman in the dark."

Robert Louis Stevenson (1850–94), poet, on Matthew Arnold, poet:

"Poor Matt. He's gone to heaven, no doubt—but he won't like God."

Frank Sullivan (1892–1976), American journalist:

"New York—A city of 7,000,000 so decadent that when I leave it I never dare look back lest I turn into salt and the conductor throw me over his shoulder for good luck."

Jeremy Thorpe (b. 1929), British Liberal politician, on a cabinet reorganization by Prime Minister Harold Macmillan:

"Greater love hath no man than this, that he lay down his friends for his life."

President Harry S. Truman (1884–1972), to Paul Hume, music critic of the *Washington Post*:

"I have just read your lousy review buried in the back pages. You sound like a frustrated old man who never made a success, an eight-ulcer man on a four-ulcer job, and all four ulcers working. I have never met you, but if I do you'll need a new nose and plenty of beefsteak and perhaps a supporter below."

Mark Twain (1835–1910), American humorist:

"I am not the editor of a newspaper and shall always try to do right and be good so that God will not make me one."

Henry van Dyke (1852–1933), American writer and clergyman:

"Jazz: music invented for the torture of imbeciles."

Oscar Wilde (1854–1900), Irish playwright:

"The man who could call a spade a spade should be compelled to use one. It is the only thing he is fit for."

Also:

"When I first saw the falls at Niagara I was disappointed in the outline. Every American bride is taken there, and the sight must be one of the earliest, if not the keenest, disappointments of American married life."

And:

"Of course America had often been discovered before Columbus, but it had always been hushed up."

On dramatist Henry Arthur Jones:

"The first rule for a young playwright to follow is not to write like Henry Arthur Jones. . . . The second and third rules are the same."

The Duke of Windsor (Edward VIII of England) (1894–1972):

"The thing that impresses me most about America is the way parents obey their children."

Virginia Woolf (1882–1941), English writer, on James Joyce:

"The work of a queasy undergraduate scratching his pimples."

Israel Zangwill (1864–1926), English novelist:

"The way Bernard Shaw believes in himself is very refreshing in these atheistic days when so many people believe in no God at all."

When a clergyman asked the British politician **George Canning** how he had enjoyed his sermon, Canning replied:

"You were brief."

"Yes," said the clergyman, "you know I avoid being tedious."

"But you were tedious," concluded Canning.

Earl Warren, U.S. Chief Justice after being Governor of California, once opened his address to a political gathering:

"I'm pleased to see such a dense crowd here tonight."

"Don't be too pleased, Governor," a voice shouted, "we ain't all dense."

Benjamin Disraeli, who was about to stand for election to the Houses of Parliament, was asked:

"On what do you propose to stand?"

"On my head," was his reply.

On the first night of one of his plays **Oscar Wilde** was receiving flowers from members of the audience in the foyer, after the play had ended. Far from wishing to congratulate him, one of his bitterest rivals pushed forward and presented him with a rotten cabbage.

"Thank you, my dear fellow," said Wilde, "every time I smell it I shall be reminded of you."

One of the Puritan fathers, who imposed the strictest discipline on his family, greeted his daughter arriving late at the breakfast table:

"Child of the Devil."

To which she replied:

"Good morning, father."

During a lawsuit **James McNeill Whistler** was questioned about a picture which he had painted in two days. Was it true that he had demanded $500 for only two days' work?

"Oh no," he replied, "I ask that for the knowledge of a lifetime."

To a friend who fell asleep while watching one of **Noel Coward's** plays, snored loudly through the whole performance and who later apologized for his behavior, the playwright replied:

"My dear fellow, don't apologize. After all, I have never bored you half as much as you have bored me."

Just as **Al Smith,** Governor of New York State, was about to begin a campaign speech a voice from the back of the hall shouted:

"Go ahead, Al. Tell 'em all you know. It won't take long."

"If I tell 'em all we both know," Smith replied, "it won't take me any longer."

When the movie company, Warner Brothers, threatened to sue **Groucho Marx,** one of the Marx Brothers, for giving his film the title *A Night in Casablanca* because it was too similar to their film *Casablanca,* Groucho answered:

"I'll sue you for using the word 'Brothers'."

Asked where he saw the role of women in society, **James Thurber** declared:

"A woman's place is in the wrong."

Thanking authors who sent him copies of their books for him to read, **Lincoln** used to add:

"Be sure I will lose no time in reading it."

Winston Churchill once received two tickets from Bernard Shaw for the opening night of his latest play, with the invitation:

"Bring a friend—if you have one."

Churchill regretted that he was engaged that night and asked for tickets for the second night: "If there is one!"

Henry Clay meeting John Randolph on a narrow sidewalk in Washington informed him:

"I, sir, do not step aside for a scoundrel."

To which Randolph replied:

"On the other hand, I always do."

During the Coronation of Queen Elizabeth II in 1953, the visiting heads of state drove through the streets of London in open carriages waving to the crowds. As the Queen of Tonga, a lady of ample proportions, passed by, a friend turned to Noel Coward and asked who the little man seated opposite her was, to which the playwright replied:

"Probably her lunch."

The 18th century British politician John Wilkes was informed by one of his constituents: "Vote for you? I'd as soon vote for the devil!"

To which he replied:

"And if your friend is not standing?"

At dinner one evening the British woman politician Bessie Braddock turned to Winston Churchill and said:

"Winston, you're drunk!"

"Bessie, you're ugly," answered Churchill. "And tomorrow morning I shall be sober."

Samuel Johnson once informed his friend and biographer **James Boswell:**

"Sir, you have but two topics, yourself and me. I am sick of both."

Once asked if life was worth living, **Mark Twain** replied:

"It depends on the liver."

When informed by a heckler at a public meeting that he, the heckler, was a Democrat, **Theodore Roosevelt** enquired:

"May I ask the gentleman why he is a Democrat?"

"My grandfather was a Democrat," answered the heckler, "my father was a Democrat, and I am a Democrat."

"My friend," said Roosevelt, "suppose your grandfather had been a jackass and your father was a jackass, what would you be?"

"A Republican!" was the immediate reply.

Invited to comment on a two-line poem, the 18th century French writer **Antoine de Rivarol** told the eager poet:

"Very nice, though there are dull stretches."

While at a cocktail party in Egypt, a function which he had been grudgingly forced to attend, **T. E. Lawrence** (Lawrence of Arabia) was approached by a lady of uncertain age, who had a reputation for trying to add celebrities to her list of social acquaintances. Deciding to use the current heat-wave as a means to engage him in conversation, she assailed Lawrence with:

"92 today, Colonel Lawrence! Imagine it! 92 today!"

"Many happy returns, madam," came the reply.

Asked by an enthusiastic fellow critic what he thought of a new production, the critic, **Alexander Woollcott** answered:

"The scenery was beautiful but the actors got in front of it. The play left a taste of lukewarm parsnip juice."

Meeting **Dorothy Parker** in a doorway, **Clare Boothe Luce** offered to let her pass through first, saying:

"Age before beauty."

In reply Miss Parker swept through the door commenting:

"Pearls before swine."

A young composer who had written two pieces of music invited the great Rossini to listen to them and say which he preferred. The young man duly played the first piece, whereupon Rossini intervened.

"You need not play any more," he said. "I prefer the other."

When **Spencer Tracy** met **Katharine Hepburn** for the first time she remarked:

"I'm afraid I'm a little tall for you, Mr. Tracy."

"Never mind, Miss Hepburn," was the reply, "I'll soon cut you down to size."

In reply to a clergyman who said he wanted to thank him for all the enjoyment he had given the world, **Groucho Marx** replied:

"And I want to thank you for all the enjoyment you've taken out of the world."

When asked the reason why he preferred sailing in non-British ships, **Somerset Maugham** answered:

"Because, in non-British ships, there's none of that nonsense about women and children first."

Asked what she wore at night, **Marilyn Monroe** replied:
   "Chanel No. 5."

After being found guilty of a criminal offense the defendant was asked whether he wished to say anything before sentence was passed.
   "Yes," he shouted, "as God is my judge I am innocent."
   "You're mistaken," the judge replied. "He isn't; I am; you aren't; six months."

A young lady seated next to the notoriously taciturn **Calvin Coolidge** at a public dinner coyly addressed him:
   "Mr. President, I have made a bet with my friends that I can make you say at least three words to me during dinner."
   "You lose," came the reply.

When informed by a lady that a certain landscape reminded her of his painting, **Whistler** replied:
   "Yes, madam, Nature is creeping up."

Commenting on a certain cantankerous Scottish historian and his equally intolerable wife, the Victorian satirist **Samuel Butler** observed:
   "It was very good of God to let Carlyle and Mrs. Carlyle marry one another and so make only two people miserable instead of four."

Commenting on an anonymous actor, **Walter Kerr** remarked:
   "He has delusions of adequacy."

A reporter who once asked the great Italian composer, **Giuseppe Verdi** for his full postal address, was told:
   "I think that Italy will be sufficient."

An arrogant young man, who was present at a dinner party at which **Dr. Samuel Johnson** was also a guest, was unwise enough to taunt the old gentleman. Ungraciously confronting his senior, he asked him:

"Tell me, Doctor, what would you give to be as young and sprightly as I am?"

"Why sir," replied Johnson, "I should almost be content to be as foolish and conceited."

While speaking at a political meeting, the Australian politician **Robert Menzies** was interrupted by a female heckler who shouted:

"I wouldn't vote for you if you were the Archangel Gabriel!"

"If I were the Archangel Gabriel, madam," answered Menzies, "you would scarcely be in my constituency."

During the Civil War a lady exclaimed effusively to **Lincoln:**

"Oh, Mr. President, I feel so sure that God is on our side, don't you?"

"Ma'am," replied Lincoln, "I am more concerned that we should be on God's side."

When asked by a despairing political colleague how he would convert the French peasantry to Rationalism, **Talleyrand** advised:

"Well, you might try getting crucified and rising again on the third day."

J. Pierpont Morgan, the financier, was once approached by a friend to whom he had frequently lent money in the past and never received repayment.

"Will you lend me your ear," his friend began . . .

"Certainly," cut in Morgan, "but nothing else."

Noel Coward was presenting one of his comedies on Broadway at the same time as an actress friend was playing the Virgin Mary in a deeply religious play called **The Miracle.** When they met some time later the actress remarked:

"I saw your play, Noel, but I am afraid I did not laugh once."

"Didn't you, darling?" replied Coward. "I saw yours and simply roared."

Whistler had been commissioned to paint the portrait of an exceedingly ugly man and, when it was finished, model and artist contemplated the work.

"Well," exclaimed the subject of the portrait, "you can't call that a great work of art."

"Perhaps not," replied Whistler, "but then you can hardly call yourself a great work of Nature."

Diogenes the Cynic was the founder of a school of philosophy which eschewed all worldly possessions. He lived in a barrel himself and it was there that he was visited one day by no less a personage than Alexander the Great. The Macedonian king stood in front of the opening to the barrel and asked the sage if there was anything he desired.

"Yes," replied Diogenes, "I should like you to stand out of my light."

Sir Winston Churchill and **Lady Astor** were notorious verbal sparring partners. On one occasion when they were seated next to each other at dinner arguing heatedly, Lady Astor turned on her adversary saying:

"Winston, if you were my husband, I should flavour your coffee with poison."

"Madam," retorted Sir Winston, "if I were your husband, I should drink it."

Asked what he thought about Western civilization, **Mahatma Gandhi** answered:

"I think it would be a very good idea."

"I buried my husband three months ago."
"Oh, I am sorry, what was the matter with him?"
"He was dead."

In his later years **Lionel Barrymore** was asked by a young reporter whether acting was as much fun for him as it used to be.

"Young man," replied Barrymore, "I am 75. Nothing is as much fun as it used to be."

Before achieving fame as a painter, **Whistler** had worked in a Government department in Washington. Reproved for continually arriving late at the office, he replied:

"It is not that I arrive late. It is the office that opens too early."

Asked whether he knew the definition of an extravagance, **Groucho Marx** answered:

"I ought to. I married one."

After an absence from Britain of ten years, a Hollywood film star returned to make a movie. She particularly asked to be photographed by the same cameraman as before.

However, when she saw the rushes, she was disappointed and said to the cameraman:

"These are not nearly as good as the ones you last took of me."

"I know, my dear," replied the cameraman, "but you must remember that I am ten years older."

Dorothy Parker, hearing the news that Calvin Coolidge had died, asked:

"How can they tell?"

Voicing his opinion of Daniel Webster, **Emerson** remarked:

"The word liberty in the mouth of Mr. Webster sounds like the word love in the mouth of a courtesan."

The dancer, **Isadora Duncan,** once suggested to **Bernard Shaw** that they should have a child together.

"Imagine," she said, "a child with my body and your brain."

"Yes," Shaw replied, "but suppose it had my body and your brain."

A friend of **Mae West's** noticing a costly necklace adorning the actress, enquired of her:

"Goodness, Mae, where did you get those beautiful pearls?"

"Never mind," replied Miss West, "but you can take it from me that goodness had nothing to do with it."

Asked in later life if her marriage to **Karl Marx** had been happy, his widow wistfully replied:

"Yes, we were happy enough, but I wish dear Karl could have spent some time acquiring capital instead of merely writing about it."

Returning the copy of a work he had been asked to read, **Dr. Samuel Johnson** said to the expectant author:

"Your manuscript is both good and original; but the part that is good is not original, and the part that is original is not good."

When a reporter asked **Marilyn Monroe**: "Did you really have nothing on when you posed for those pictures?" she smiled at him and replied:

"Oh no, I had the radio on."

When **Whistler** was asked by a lady where he had been born, he told her that it was in Lowell, Massachusetts.

"Why, Mr. Whistler," she mockingly reproved him, "what possessed you to be born in a place like that?"

"The explanation is quite simple, madam, I wished to be near my mother."

Trapped at a party by an overbearing woman reporter, who addressed him: "Dear Mr. Marx. We met at Mrs. X's, I'm sure you remember me?"

Groucho Marx answered: "I never forget a face, but in your case I'll make an exception."

Reflecting on the fortunes of life a fellow actor said to **John Barrymore**: "Well, we live and learn."

To which Barrymore replied: "Yes. And then we die and forget it all."

Invited to comment on the reports of his death that were circulating, **Mark Twain** replied:

"The reports of my death have been greatly exaggerated!"

Cross-examining a hostile witness, the famous lawyer **Edward Carson** enquired:

"You drink, don't you?"

"That's my business," snapped the witness.

"Have you any other business?"

When a barber brightly asked **George S. Kaufman** how he liked his hair cut, the playwright replied:
"In perfect silence."

After returning from church one morning **Calvin Coolidge** was asked by his wife about the sermon. He told her it had been about sin.
"Well," demanded Mrs. Coolidge, "what did the preacher have to say about sin?"
The President remained wrapped in thought for several minutes before finally uttering:
"He's against it."

Told by a notorious bore:
"I passed your house yesterday."
Oscar Wilde's reply was:
"Oh, thank you so much."

Dorothy Parker and a woman friend were discussing a mutual acquaintance.
"You must admit," said the friend, "that he is always courteous to his inferiors."
"Where does he find them?" asked Miss Parker.

On one occasion when **General Charles de Gaulle** called a hurried meeting of the Free French National Committee in Algiers, one of his ministers arrived in shorts and sneakers, having received the summons while he was on the beach. Eyeing him coldly, de Gaulle enquired:
"Haven't you forgotten something?"
"What?" the minister asked.
"Your hoop," replied de Gaulle.

Lady Astor, the first woman member of the British Parliament, was interrupted in the middle of one of her speeches by a heckler who shouted:

"Your husband's a millionaire, isn't he?"

"I hope so," she replied, "that's why I married him."

A friend commented to **Dorothy Parker:** "Isn't your dress a little too young for you, dear?"

She replied: "Do you think so, dear? I think yours suits you perfectly. It always has."

When **Khrushchev** was still leader of the Soviet Union he addressed a large audience on the subject of the iniquities of Joseph Stalin. A voice cried out from the back of the hall: "You were one of his colleagues, why didn't you stop him?"

No one moved in the awful silence that followed. Glaring round the crowded hall, Khrushchev bellowed: "Who said that?"

Still not a man moved and the tension was becoming unbearable, when Khrushchev quietly said: "Now you know why."

An infatuated young man was sending his girl friend a cable which read:

"Ozzy loves his Woozy Woozy Woozy."

"You can have another 'Woozy' without it costing any more," said the desk clerk.

"No, thanks," replied the young man. "I think that would sound rather silly."

Answering a lady who had asked him whether genius was hereditary, **Whistler** said:

"I cannot tell you, madam. Heaven has granted me no offspring."

A lady in an advanced state of pregnancy was approached by the neighborhood gossip, who enquired:

"Excuse me, but are you going to have a baby?"

"Oh, no," was the caustic reply, "I'm just carrying this round for a friend."

During the Boer War in South Africa, **Whistler** was discussing a recent engagement with a friend who was extolling the military merits of the commander of the British forces. The friend claimed that the general had withdrawn from the action "without losing a man, a gun, or a flag," to which Whistler added:

"Or a minute."

"What do you think of marriage as an institution?"

"I think it's fine for people who like living in institutions."

Concluding his explanation of a battle plan to his staff, **Napoleon** said:

"If my orders are obeyed to the letter, we shall win the day."

One of the Marshals piously uttered: "God willing, sire." To which the emperor retorted:

"God has nothing to do with it."

An irritating passenger asked an air hostess:

"How often do aircraft of this type crash?" to which the hostess replied: "Only once."

Asked by a reporter whether he could play the violin, **George Burns** replied:

"I don't know; I've never tried."

When a lady congratulated **Dr. Johnson** on the fact that his dictionary contained no "naughty" words, he thanked her, enquiring:
"And how do you know that, Madam, unless you have read all through it looking for them?"

Lady Margot Asquith was attending a Hollywood party at which **Jean Harlow** was also present. Noticing the wife of the British statesman, the actress approached her and said:
"Why, you are Margott Asquith, aren't you?"
"No, my dear," the peeress replied icily. "The 't' is silent, as in Harlow."

Admiring one of **Whistler's** witticisms, **Oscar Wilde** said appreciatively:
"I wish I'd said that."
"You will, Oscar, you will," Whistler replied.

Asked by a reporter how many husbands she had had, **Zsa Zsa Gabor** enquired:
"You mean apart from my own?"

Asked to spell his name by a telephone operator, a certain professor obliged accordingly:
"B for Brontosaurus; R for Rhizophoroceae; O for Opisthothele; W for Willugbaeya and N for Nucifraga."

Hearing the announcement of the precociously young Thomas Dewey's candidacy for the Republican Presidential nomination, Secretary of the Interior **Harold L. Ickes** remarked:
"Dewey has thrown his diaper into the ring."

When a hotel receptionist called **Edna Ferber's** room phone and asked:

"I beg your pardon, Miss Ferber, but is there a gentleman in your room?"

The authoress replied:

"I don't know. Wait a minute and I'll ask him."

After everyone was seated at an ambassadorial banquet, one of the lady guests complained rather too loudly that, according to the official order of precedence, she ought to be seated next to the host. She was found to be right and several of the other guests were forced to move down to make room for her next to the ambassador.

Slightly abashed at the fuss she had caused, the lady said to the ambassador:

"You and your wife must find these questions of precedence extremely troublesome."

"Not really," her host replied, "we have found by experience that the people who matter don't mind and the people who mind don't matter."

A man who had been spending a very convivial evening with a group of male friends telephoned his wife at 2 A.M. to tell her that he would be home late.

"I hope I'm not disturbing you, dear," he said when he heard her voice at the other end.

"Oh no," she replied. "I had to get up to answer the phone in any case."

Asked to what he attributed his advanced age of seventy, the British conductor **Sir Malcolm Sargent** replied:

"Well, I suppose I must attribute it to the fact that I haven't died yet."

The 18th century politician and rake **John Wilkes** was arguing with a fellow politician, Lord Sandwich, who exclaimed:
   "Sir, you will die either of the pox or on the gallows."
   To which Wilkes replied: "Depending on whether I em-
brace your mistress or your principles."

A young poet, Laman Blanchard, sent **Charles Dickens** one
of his poems for inclusion in one of Dickens's publications.
The poem was called "Orient Pearls at Random Strung,"
but it was returned by Dickens with the note:
   "Dear Mr. Blanchard—too much string.

                                                 Yours, C. D."

III
Grave
Moments

The "Guinness Book" says that Johann Heinrich Karl Thieme, sexton of Aldenburg in Germany, dug 23,311 graves during a career which spanned half-a-century and ended with his own death in 1826. Assuming he could read, Thieme, as the world's busiest grave-digger, probably read more tombstones than anyone—except perhaps me.

I have always enjoyed walking around graveyards—it's not such fun being carried round them—and reading the inscriptions on the gravestones. The epitaphs in this chapter come from both sides of the Atlantic. Most of them have actually been seen inscribed on a gravestone—although a few were written for publication rather than graveyard inscription—and where the location of the tombstone is known it is given.

In memory of
Mr Peter Daniels
1688–1746.
Beneath this stone, this lump of clay,
Lies Uncle Peter Daniels,
Who too early in the month of May
Took off his winter flannels.

Medway, Massachusetts

Here lies the Earl of Suffolk's fool, men called
  him Dicky Pearce,
His folly served to make men laugh when wit and mirth
  were scarce.
Poor Dick alas is dead and gone, what signifies to cry.
Dickys enough are still behind to laugh at by and by.

Berkley, Gloucestershire, England

Here lies
Lester Moore
Four slugs
from a 44
no Les
no more

Tombstone, Arizona

Brigham Young
Born on this spot
1801
A man of great courage
and superb equipment.

Whitingham, Vermont

Sarah Shute
1803–1840
Here lies, cut down like unripe fruit,
The wife of Deacon Amos Shute.
She died of drinking too much coffee,
Anno Dominy eighteen forty.

Canaan, New Hampshire

Here lies in a horizontal position the outside case of
Thomas Hinde
clock and watch maker.
Who departed this life wound up
in hope of being taken in hand
by his Maker and being
thoroughly cleaned repaired and
set a-going in the world to come.
On the 15th of August 1836
in the nineteenth year of his life.

Bolsover, Derbyshire, England

Sacred to the memory of Anthony Drake,
Who died for peace and quietness sake;
His wife was constantly scolding and scoffin',
So he sought for repose in a twelve dollar coffin.

Burlington, Massachusetts

M. S. Donald Robertson
Born 1st of January 1785
Died 4th of June 1848
Aged 63 years.

He was a peaceable man, and, to all appearance a sincere Christian. His death was very much regretted—which was caused by the stupidity of Lawrence Tulloch of Clotherton who sold him nitre instead of Epsom salts by which he was killed in the space of three hours after taking a dose of it.

Cross Kirk, Shetland, England

Here lies
Father and Mother
and Sister and I
We all died within the space of one short year
They all be buried at Wimble, except I
And I be buried here.

Nettlebed, Oxfordshire, England

Here lies Ann Mann;
She lived an old maid and
She died an Old Mann.

Bath Abbey, England

Here lies my wife in earthly mold,
Who when she lived did naught but scold.
Peace! wake her not, for now she's still,
She had; but now I have my will.

Bayfield, Mississippi

He called Bill Smith a liar.

Cripplecreek, Colorado

In remembrance of that prodigy in nature
Daniel Lambert
A native of Leicester
who was possessed of an
excellent & convivial hind
& in personal greatness
had no competitor.
He measured 3 ft 1 inch
round the leg, nine ft 4 in
round the body & weigh'd
52 stones 11 lb
He departed this life on the
21st of June 1809 aged 39 yrs.
As a testimony of respect
this stone was erected
by his friends in Leicester.

Stamford, Lincolnshire, England

Erected to the memory of
John Philips
accidentally shot as a mark
of affection by his brother.

Saratoga, New York

Here lies the bones of Richard Lawton,
Whose death, alas! was strangely brought on.
Trying his corns one day to mow off,
His razor slipped and cut his toe off,
His toe, or, rather what it grew to,
An inflammation quickly flew to.
Which took, alas! to mortifying,
And was the cause of Richard's dying.

Plymouth, Massachusetts

Here lies
John James Cook
of Newby
Who was a faithful
servant
to his master
and an
upright downright
honest man
1760.

Ripon, Yorkshire, England

In this grave ye see before ye
Lyes berried up a desmal story.
A young maiden crossed in love
And tooketh to the realms above.
But he that crossed her
I should say
Deserves to go the other way.

Pentewan, Cornwall, England

Here lie I bereft of breath
Because a cough carried me off;
Then a coffin they carried me off in.

Boston (Mass.) Granary Burying-Ground

Sacred to the memory of
Elisha Philbrook and his wife Sarah
Beneath these stones do lie,
Back to back, my wife and I!
When the last trumpet the air shall fill,
If she gets up, I'll just lie still.

Sargentville, Maine

Here lies the clay of Mitchell Coots,
Whose feet yet occupy his boots.
His soul has gone—we know not where
It landed, neither do we care.
He slipped the joker up his sleeve
With vile intention to deceive,
And when detected, tried to jerk
His gun, but didn't get his work
In with sufficient swiftness, which
Explains the presence here of Mitch.
At Gabriel's trump if he should wake,
He'll mighty likely try to take
The trump with that same joker he
Had sleeved so surreptitiously
And which we placed upon his bier
When we concealed his body here.

Lost Creek, Colorado

This tombstone is a Milestone; ha, how so,
Because beneath lies Miles, who's miles below.

Selby, Yorkshire, England

Here under this sod and under these trees
Is buried the body of Solomon Pease.
But here in his hole lies only his pod
His soul is shelled out and gone up to God.

Falkirk, Scotland

Beneath this stone, a lump of clay
Lies Arabella Young
Who on the 21st of May
Began to hold her tongue.

Hatfield, Massachusetts

Beneath this stone our baby lays,
He neither cries nor hollers,
He lived just one and twenty days,
And cost us forty dollars.

Burlington, Vermont

Stranger pause, my tale attend,
And learn the cause of Hannah's end.
Across the world the wind did blow,
She ketched a cold that laid her low.
We shed a lot of tears 'tis true,
But life is short—aged 82.

Bayfield, Mississippi

Here lies the body of our Anna
Done to death by a banana.
It wasn't the fruit that laid her low
But the skin of the thing that made her go.

Enosburg, Vermont

Underneath this pile of stones
Lies all that's left of Sally Jones.
Her name was Briggs, it was not Jones,
But Jones was used to rhyme with stones.

Skaneateles, New York

Beneath these stones
Lies William Jones,
The bailiff and the Bum;
When he died,
The devil cried,
Come, Billy, come.

Sheffield, Yorkshire, England

Here lies the bones of my boy Fritz,
The Lord killed him with ague fits.
He was too good to live with me,
So He took him home to live with He.

Germantown, Pennsylvania

Here, beneath this stone, there lies,
Waiting a summons to the skies,
The body of Samuel Jinking;
He was an honest Christian man,
His fault was that he took, and ran
Suddenly to drinking.
Whoever reads this tablet o'er,
Take warning now, and drink no more.

Augusta, Maine

Here lyes
Sydney Snyder
1803–1823
The wedding day decided was,
The wedding wine provided,
But ere the day did come along
He'd drunk it and died, did.
Ah, Sidney! Sidney!

Providence, Rhode Island

Here Betsy Brown her body lies,
Her soul is flying to the skies.
While here on earth she ofttimes spun
Six hundred skeins from sun to sun,
And wove one day, her daughter brags,
Two hundred pounds of carpet rags.

Winslow, Maine

Here lies the body of
Lady O'Looney
Great niece of Burke.
Commonly called the sublime
She was bland, passionate
and deeply religious, also
she painted in water colours
and sent several pictures
to the Exhibition.
She was first cousin to
Lady Jones
and of such is the
Kingdom of Heaven.

Pewsey, Wiltshire, England

Here lies
John Taggart
of honest fame,
of stature low
&
a leg lame.
Content was he
with portion small
kept a shop in Wigtown
&
that's all

Wigtown, Galloway, Scotland

Sacred to the memory of
Jared Bates
who died Aug. the 6th 1800.
His widow, aged 24, lives at 7 Elm
Street, has every qualification for a
good wife, and yearns to be comforted.

Lincoln, Maine

Here lieth
Martin Elphinstone
who with his sword
did cut in sunder
the daughter of
Sir Harry Crispe
who did his daughter marry
She was fat and fulsome
But men will sometimes
Eat bacon with their bean
And love the fat
As well as lean.

Alnwick, Northumberland, England

In memory of
Charles Ward
who died May 1770
aged 63 years.
A dutiful son
A loving brother and
An affectionate husband

    NB This stone was not erected by Susan his wife. She erected a stone to John Salter her second husband forgetting the affection of Charles Ward, her first husband.

Lowestoft, Suffolk, England

Cynthia Stevens
1742–1776
Here lies Cynthia, Stevens' wife,
She lived six years in calm and strife.
Death came at last and set her free,
I was glad and so was she.

Hollis, New Hampshire

Amos Shute
1789–1842
He heard the angels calling him
From the Celestial Shore,
He flapped his wings and away he went
To make one angel more.

Canaan, New Hampshire

O Cruel Death how could you be so unkind
To take him before and leave me behind
You should have taken the two of us if either
Which would have been more pleasing to the survivor.

Birmingham, England

Here lieth
Mary—the wife of John Ford
We hope her soul is gone to the Lord
But if for Hell she has changed this life
She had better be there than be John Ford's wife
1790

Potterne, Wiltshire, England

Here lies the body of
J. Wesley Webb
A firm believer in the Lord
Jesus Christ, Jeffersonian Democracy
and the M. E. Church.

Huntington, West Virginia

On a Thursday she was born,
On a Thursday she made a bride,
On a Thursday put to bed,
On a Thursday broke her leg, and
On a Thursday died.

Church Stretton, Shropshire, England

Neuralgia worked on Mrs Smith
Till neath the sod it laid her.
She was a worthy Methodist
And served as a crusader.

Skaneateles, New York

My wife from me departed
And robbed me like a knave;
Which caused me broken hearted
To sink into the grave.
My children took an active part,
To doom me did contrive;
Which stuck a dagger in my heart
That I could not survive.

Stowe, Vermont

Old Thomas Mulvaney lies here
His mouth ran from ear to ear.
Reader, tread lightly on this wonder,
For if he yawns you're gone to thunder.

Middlefield, Massachusetts

To the four husbands of
Miss Ivy Saunders
1790, 1794, 1808, 18??
Here lie my husbands, One, Two, Three
Dumb as men could ever be.
As for my Fourth, well, praise be God,
He bides for a little above the sod.
Alex, Ben, Sandy were the first three's names,
And to make things tidy I'll add his—James.

Shutesbury, Massachusetts

Here lies the body of John Eldred,
At least, he will be when he's dead;
But now at this time he is alive,
The 14th of August, Sixty-five.

A churchyard in Oxfordshire, England

Of seven sons the Lord his father gave,
He was the fourth who found a watery grave.
Fifteen days had passed since the circumstance occurred,
When his body was found and decently interred.

South Dennis, Massachusetts

Sacred to the memory of
Henry Harris
Born June 27, 1821, of Henry Harris
and Jane, His Wife. Died on the 4th
of May, 1837, by the kick of a
Colt in his bowels.
Peaceable and quiet, a friend to his
father and mother, and respected by all
who knew him, and went to the world
where horses do not kick, where sorrow
and weeping is no more.

Williamsport, Pennsylvania

Here lies the body of Molly Dickie,
the wife of Hall Dickie tailor.
Two great physicians first
My loving husband tried
To cure my pain—
In vain;
At last he got a third,
And then I died.

Cheltenham, Gloucestershire, England

In memory of
Robert Baxter
of Farhouse
Who died October 4th 1796
Aged 56 years
All you that please these lines to read
It will cause a tender heart to bleed
I murdered was upon the fell
And by a man I know full well
By bread and butter which he'd laid—
I being harmless was betray'd
I hope he will rewarded be
That laid the poison there for me.

Knaresdale, Northumberland, England

Thomas Woodcock
Here lie the remains of Thomas Woodhen
The most amiable of husbands and excellent of men.
His real name was Woodcock
but it wouldn't come in rhyme.

Dunoon, Scotland

In memory of
Mrs Alpha White
Weight 309 lbs
Open wide ye heavenly gates
That lead to the heavenly shore;
Our father suffered in passing through
And mother weighs much more.

Lee, Massachusetts

Vast strong was I, but yet did dye,
And in my grave asleep I lye
My grave is steam'd round about.
Yet I hope the Lord will find me out.

West Grinstead, Sussex, England

Sacred to the memory of
John Walker,
the only son of Benjamin and Ann Walker,
engineer and palisade maker
died September 23, 1832, aged 36 years.
Farewell, my wife and father dear,
No engine powers now do I fear;
My glass is run, my work is done,
And now my head lies quiet here.
Tho' many an engine I've set up,
And got great praise from men;
I made them work on British ground,
And on the roaring main.
My engine's stopped, my valves are bad,
And lies so deep within;
No engineer could here be found
To put the new ones in.
But Jesus Christ converted me,
And took me up above;
I hope once more to meet once more,
And sing redeeming love.

Bridgford-on-the-Hill, Nottinghamshire, England

Of children in all she bore twenty-four:
Thank the Lord there will be no more.

Canterbury, Kent, England

Here lyeth ye body of
Sarah Bloomfield,
Aged 74
Cut off in blooming yuthe we can but pity.

Yarmouth, Norfolk, England

This stone was raised by Sarah's lord,
Not Sarah's virtues to record—
For they're well known to all the town—
But it was raised to keep her down.

Kilmurry, Ireland

Fear God,
Keep the commandments,
and
Don't attempt to climb a tree,
For that's what caused the death of me.

Eastwell, Kent, England

Thomas Alleyn and his Two Wives, ob.1650:
Death here advantage hath of life I spye,
One husband with two wives at once may lye.

Witchingham, Norfolk, England

Grim Death took me without any warning
I was well at night, and dead in the morning.

Sevenoaks, Kent, England

Charity, wife of Gideon Bligh,
Underneath this stone doth lie.
Nought was she e'er known to do
That her husband told her to.

Churchyard in Devonshire, England

Here lies the body of Alexander MacPherson,
Who was a very extraordinary person;
He was two yards high in his stocking feet,
And kept his accoutrements clean and neat.
He was slew
At the battle of Waterloo,
Plump through
The gullet; it went in at his throat
And came out at the back of his coat.

Churchyard in Scotland

Solomon Towslee Jr.
who was killed in Pownal Vt. July 15, 1846
while repairing to grind a scythe on a stone
attached to the gearing in the Woollen Factory.
He was entangled. His death was sudden and awful.

Pownal, Vermont

In memory of
Mr Nath Parks, aged 19,
who on 21st March 1794 being out hunting
and concealed in a ditch was casually shot
by Mr Luther Frank.

Elmwood Cemetery, Holyoke, Massachusetts

Sacred to the memory of Hester Fisher of Waterhouse, also of Anne Rothery wife of N. P. Rothery, R.N. and of Elizabeth Ann Rothery their daughter, who were unfortunately drowned at Chepstow on the evening of Saturday Septr. 20th 1812, after hearing a sermon from Philippians 1st chapter 21st verse.

Monkton Combe, Somerset, England

Devoted Christian mother who whipped Sherman's bummers with scalding water while trying to take her dinner pot which contained a hambone being cooked for her soldier boys.

Pleasant Grove Cemetery, Raleigh, N. Carolina

Here lies a man of good repute
Who wore a No. 16 boot.
'Tis not recorded how he died,
But sure it is, that open wide,
The gates of heaven must have been
To let such monstrous feet within.

Keeseville, New York

Here lies the body of
Samuel Young
who came here and died for the benefit of his health.

Ventnor, Isle of Wight, England

Here lies the body of John Mound
Lost at sea and never found.

Winslow, Maine

Here lies the man Richard,
And Mary his wife;
Their surname was Pritchard,
They lived without strife;
And the reason was plain,
They abounded in riches,
They had no care or pain,
And his wife wore the breeches.

Chelmsford, Essex, England

Here lies the body of
Mary Ellis
daughter of Thomas Ellis and Lydia, his wife, of this parish.
She was a virgin of virtuous character & most promising hopes
She died on the 3rd of June 1609 aged one hundred and
nineteen.

Leigh, Essex, England

They lived and they laugh'd while they were able
And at last was obliged to knock under the table.

Newbury, Berkshire, England

We	Must	All	Die
Must	We	Die	All
All	Die	We	Must
Die	All	Must	We.

Bacton, Norfolk, England

Sacred to the memory of
Nathaniel Goldbold, Esq.
Inventor and Proprietor of that excellent medicine
The Vegetable Balsam for the cure of Consumption
and Asthmas.
He departed this life the 17th day of Decr., 1799.
His ashes are here, his fame everywhere.

Godalming, Surrey, England

Here lies I—
Jonathan Fry—
Killed by a sky-
Rocket in my eye-
Socket.

Frodsham, Cheshire, England

Shoot-'em-up-Jake
Ran for sheriff, 1872
Ran for sheriff, 1876
Buried, 1876.

Boot Hill Cemetery, Dodge City, Kansas

Censure not rashly though nature's apt to halt,
No woman's born that dies without fault.

Islington, London, England

Sudden and unexpected was the end,
Of our esteemed and beloved friend.
He gave all his friends a sudden shock,
By one day falling into Sunderland Dock.

Whitby, Yorkshire, England

Sacred to the memory of inestimable worth of unrivalled
excellence and virtue, N.R., whose ethereal parts became
seraphic, May 25th, 1767.

Litchfield, Connecticut

Here lies one who for medicine would not give
A little gold; and so his life he lost:
I fancy that he'd wish again to live
Did he but know how much his funeral cost.

Dorchester-on-Thames, Oxfordshire, England

Here lie I by the chancel door,
Here lie I because I'm poor,
The farther in, the more you pay,
Here lie I as warm as they.

Kingsbridge, Devon, England

Beneath these green trees rising to the skies,
The planter of them, Isaac Greentrees, lies;
The time shall come when these green trees shall fall,
And Isaac Greentrees rise above them all.
Harrow, Middlesex, England

Here lies John Ross
Kicked by a Hoss.
Jersey, Channel Islands, England

In memory of
John Smith, who met
weirlent death neer this spot
18 hundred and 40 too. He was shot
by his own pistol. It was not one of the
new kind but a old fashioned brass barrel,
and of such is the Kingdom of Heaven.
Sparta Diggins, California

Here lies Robert Trollop,
Who made the stones roll up:
When death took his soul up,
His body filled the hole up.
Gateshead, Durham, England

Played five aces,
Now playing the harp.
Boot Hill Cemetery, Dodge City, Kansas

The Lord saw good, I was lopping off wood
And down fell from the tree
I met with a check, and broke my neck
And so Death lopped off me.
Ockham, Surrey, England

Honest John
's dead and gone.

Worcester, England

Here lies the body of Edward Hide,
We laid him here because he died.
We had rather
It had been his father.
If it had been his sister,
We should not have missed her.
But since 'tis honest Ned,
No more shall be said.

Storrington, Sussex, England

Here lies buried in the tomb,
A constant sufferer from salt rheum,
Which finally in truth did pass
To spotted erysipelas.
A husband brave, a father true,
Here he lies; and so must you.

Baton Rouge, Louisiana

How shocking to the human mind
The log did him to powder grind.
God did commit his soul away
His summings we must all obey.

Old Burial Ground, Pittsford, Vermont

From earth my body first arose,
But here to earth again it goes
I never desire to have it more
To plague me as it did before.

Llangerrig, Powys, Wales

Here lieth the body of Martha Dias
Always busy and not very pious;
Who lived the age of threescore and ten
And gave to worms what she refused to men.
Churchyard in Shropshire, England

Here lies the body of William Smith; and what is
somewhat rarish
He was born, bred and hanged in this parish.
Penryn, Cornwall, England

This blooming youth in health most fair
To his uncle's mill-pond did repair
Undressed himself and so plunged in
But never did come out again.
Center Cemetery, Plainsfield, Vermont

Bury me not when I am dead
Lay me not down in a dusty bed
I could not bear the life down there
With earth worms creeping through my hair.
Winsted, Connecticut

Here lies poor, but honest
Bryan Tunstall;
He was a most expert angler,
until Death, envious of his Merit,
threw out his line, hook'd him,
and landed him here the 21st of April 1790.
Ripon, Yorkshire, England

This gallant young man gave up his life
in the attempt to save a perishing lady.
Bodmin, Cornwall, England

Sacred to the memory
Of Miss Martha Gwynne
Who was so very pure within,
She burst the outward shell of sin
And hatched herself a cherubim.

St. Albans, Hertfordshire, England

Here lies the body of Susan Lowder
Who burst while drinking a Seidlitz powder.
Called from this world to her Heavenly Rest
She should have waited till it effervesced. 1798

Burlington, New Jersey

Erected to the memory of
John MacFarlane
Drown'd in the Water of Leith
By a few affectionate friends.

Edinburgh, Scotland

Lord, she is Thin.

Presbyterian church, Cooperstown, New York

Ruth S. Kibbs, wife of
Alvin J. Stanton
May 5, 1861
Apr 5, 1904
The Lord don't make any mistakes.

South Plymouth, New York

Let the wind go free
Wher'er thou be
For 'twas the wind
That killed me.

Leyland, Lancashire, England

In memory of
Charles H. Salmon,
who was born September 10th, 1858.

He grew, waxed strong, and developed into a noble son and loving brother. He came to his death on the 12th of October, 1884, by the hand of a careless drug clerk and two excited doctors, at 12 o'clock at night in Kansas City.

Morristown, New Jersey

Dorothy Cecil.
Unmarried as yet.

Wimbledon, London, England

Gone to be an angle.

Lieutenant John Walker Cemetery,
White Horn, Tennessee

Once ruddy and plump
But now a pale lump,
Here lies Johnny Crump
Who wished his neighbour no evil;
What though by death's thump,
He is laid on his rump,
Yet up he shall jump,
When he hears the last trump,
And triumph o'er death and the devil.

Churchyard in Worcestershire, England

Died of grief
Caused by a neighbor
Now rests in peace.

Palm Springs, California

Here lie the bones
of Joseph Jones
Who ate while he was able;
But once o'er fed
He dropt down dead,
And fell beneath the table.
When from the tomb
To meet his doom
He rises amidst sinners:
Since he must dwell
In heav'n or hell
Take him—which gives best dinners.

Wolverhampton, Staffordshire, England

For the other fellow.

Elm Lawn Cemetery, Bay City, Michigan

Dear Friends and companions all
Pray warning take by me;
Don't venture on the ice too far
As 'twas the death of me.

Reigate, Surrey, England

Here lies Jane Smith, wife of Thomas Smith, marble cutter. This monument was erected by her husband as a tribute to her memory and a specimen of his work. Monuments of the same style 350 dollars.

Springdale, Ohio

My husband promised me
that my body should be
cremated but other
influences prevailed.

Glendale Cemetery, Cardington, Ohio

Jonathan Richardson, 1872, aged 82, Who never sacrificed his reason at the altar of superstition's God, who never believed that Jonah swallowed the whale.

East Thompson, Connecticut

The mortal remains of
John Brindle;
After an evil life of 64 years
Died June 18th 1822,
And lies at rest beneath this stone.

London, England

Asa Whitcomb,
A pillow of the settlement.

Barnard, Vermont

Here lies Jemmy Little, a carpenter industrious,
A very good-natured man, but somewhat blusterous.
When that his little wife his authority withstood,
He took a little stick and bang'd her as he would.
His wife, now left alone, her loss does so deplore,
She wishes Jemmy back to bang her a little more;
For now he's dead and gone this fault appears so small,
A little thing would make her think it was no fault at all.

Portsmouth, Hampshire, England

Julia Adams.
Died of thin shoes,
April 17th, 1839, aged 19 years.

New Jersey

Epitaph for a famous Long Island huntsman:
I always got a bear here.

Here lies the body of
Dr. Hayward—
a man who never voted.
Of such is the kingdom of Heaven.

Churchyard in Ohio

Here lies a careful, saving wife,
A tender, nursing mother;
A neighbour free from brawl and strife,
A pattern for all other.

Warrington, Cheshire, England

When Spring was seen my life was green
For I was blithe and young
When summer smiled my hopes beguiled,
My heart was hale and strong.
When Autumn crowned with fruits came round
I entertained no fear,
There rose at last a Wintry blast
And then they laid me here.

Stanton, Isle of Man, England

What faults you've seen in me, strive to avoid,
Search your own hearts, and you'll be well employed.

Rudston, Yorkshire, England

Here lie several of the Sauderses of this parish.
Further particulars the last day will disclose. Amen.

Tetbury, Gloucestershire, England

I am amazed that death, that tyrant grim,
Should think on me, who never thought on him.

Cambridge, England

In memory of
The Snellings
Man and Wife.
In this cold bed, here consummated are
The second nuptials of the happy pair,
Whom envious Death once parted, but in vain,
For now himself has made them one again;
Here wedded in the grave, and 'tis but just,
That they that were one flesh, should be one dust.

Canterbury, Kent, England

Within this little house, three Houses lie,
John House, James House, the short-lived twins and I,
Anne, wife of John House, once the dear loved wife
Who lost mine own, to give these babes their life.
We three, though dead, yet speak to keep in my mind
The husband, father, whom we left behind.
We were but House and only made of clay:
When we were called we could no longer stay,
But were laid here to take our rest and ease,
By Death, who taketh whom and where he please.

Langford, Oxfordshire, England

Here sleep thirteen together in one tomb,
And all these great yet quarrel not for room.

Blatherwycke, Northamptonshire, England

She was a lady of spiritual and cultivated mind, and her
death was instantaneous, arising from fright occasioned by a
violent attack made upon her house door by three or four
men in a state of intoxication with a view to disturb the
peaceful inmates in the dead of night.

Long Buckby, Northamptonshire, England

Here lieth the body of
William Strutton
of Paddington, buried May 18, 1734, who had by his first wife 28 children, and by a second wife 17, own father to 45, grandfather to 86, great-grandfather to 97, and great-great-grandfather to 23; in all, 251.

Heydon, Suffolk, England

In honoured memory of
Sarah J. Rooke
Telephone Operator
Who perished in the flood waters
of the Dry Cimarron at Folsom
New Mexico, August 27, 1908
while at the switchboard
warning others of the danger.
With heroic devotion she glorified
her calling by sacrificing her own
life that others might live.

Folsom, New Mexico

Neglected by his doctor,
Ill treated by his nurse,
His brother robbed the widow,
Which made it all the worse.

Dulverton, Somerset, England

Here lies the body of Richard Hind,
Who was neither ingenious, sober or kind.

Cheshunt, Hertfordshire, England

Here lyeth ye body of Martyn Hyde,
He fell down a midden and grievously dy'd.
James Hyde his brother fell down another,
They now lie interr'd side by side.

Here lies a lewd fellow
Who while he drew breath
In the midst of life
Was in quest of Death
Which he quickly obtained
For it cost him his life
for being in bed
With another man's wife.

To Lem S. Frame, who during his life shot 89 Indians, whom
the Lord delivered into his hands, and who was looking forward to making up his hundred before the end of the year,
when he fell asleep in Jesus at his house at Hawk's Ferry,
March 2, 1843.

Sacred to the memory of
Major James Brush
who was killed by the accidental discharge of
a pistol by his orderly.
14th April 1831
Well done thou good and faithful servant

Here lies poor Charlotte
Who died no harlot—
But in her virginity
At the age of nineteen
In this vicinity
Rare to be found or seen

Here lies
John Higley
whose father and mother were
drowned in the passage from America.
Had they both lived
they would have been buried here.

Here lie I Martin Elginbrodde
Hae mercy on my soul Lord God
As I wad so were I Lord God
And ye were Martin Elginbrodde

Epitaph on John Keats, by the poet himself:
Here lies one whose name was writ in water

Epitaph for a gamekeeper:
My gun's discharged
My ball is gone
My powder spent,
My work is done.
Those panting deer
I've left behind
May now have time
To gain the wind,
Since I, who oft have
Chased them o'er
The verdant plains,
Am now no more.

Here lies
James Earl
the pugilist
who on the 11th of April 1788
gave in

Epitaph on a dentist:
Stranger, approach this spot with gravity;
John Brown is filling his last cavity.

Epitaph for a man killed by falling from his horse:
Betwixt the stirrup and the ground
Mercy I asked, mercy I found.

Epitaph on a pessimist:
I'm Smith of Stoke, aged sixty odd,
I've lived without a dame
From youth-time on: and would to God
My dad had done the same.

Epitaph on a fellow, Trinity College, Cambridge:
Here lies a Doctor of Divinity;
He was a Fellow too of Trinity:
He knew as much about Divinity,
As other Fellows do of Trinity.

Epitaph of Captain Underwood, who was drowned:
Here lies free from blood and slaughter
Once Underwood—now under water.

Epitaph on Thomas Kemp who was hanged for stealing sheep:
Here lies the body of Thomas Kemp,
Who lived by wool and died by hemp;
There nothing would suffice the glutton
But with the fleece to steal the mutton;
Had he but worked and lived uprighter,
He'd ne'er been hung for a sheepbiter.

Epitaph for one who was struck by lightning:
Here lies a man who was killed by lightning
He died when his prospects seemed to be brightening.
He might have cut a flash in this world of trouble,
But the flash cut him, and he lies in the stubble.

**Epitaph for Susan Blake, composed at her request
by St. Thomas More:**
Good Susan Blake in royal state
Arrived at last at Heaven's gate.
(Some years later he added):
But Peter met her with a club
And knocked her back to Beelzebub.

**Epitaph for Oliver Goldsmith, English dramatist,
written by David Garrick, English actor:**
Here lies Nolly Goldsmith, for shortness call'd Noll,
Who wrote like an angel, but talk'd like poor Poll.

**Epitaph intended for the monument of William Whitehead,
English Poet Laureate:**
Beneath this stone a Poet Laureate lies,
-Nor great, nor good, nor foolish, nor yet wise;
Not meanly humble, nor yet swell'd with pride,
He simply liv'd—and just as simply died:
Each year his Muse produc'd a Birth-Day Ode,
Compos'd with flattery in the usual mode:
For this, and but for this, to George's praise,
The Bard was pension'd and received the bays.

Epitaph by Alexander Pope on two lovers killed by lightning:
Here lie two poor lovers, who had the mishap
Tho' very chased people, to die of the clap.

Epitaph for Viscount Castlereagh, written by Byron:
Posterity will ne'er survey
A nobler grave than this:
Here lie the bones of Castlereagh:
Stop, traveller, and piss.

Epitaph for an Irish priest:
Here I lie for the last time,
Lying has been my pastime,
And now I've joined the Heavenly choir
I hope I still may play the lyre.

Epitaph on a pair of English lovers:
Here lies John Hughes and Sarah Drew.
Perhaps you'll say what's that to you?
Believe me, friend, much may be said
On this poor couple that are dead.
On Sunday next they should have married;
But see how oddly things have carry'd,
On Thursday last it rain'd and lighten'd,
These tender lovers sadly frighten'd
Shelter'd beneath the cocking hay
In hopes to pass the storm away.
But the bold thunder found them out
(Commission'd for that end no doubt)
And seizing on their trembling breath,
Consign'd them to the shades of death.
Who knows if 'twas not kindly done?
For had they seen the next year's sun,
A beaten wife and cockold swain
Had jointly curs'd the marriage chain.
Now they are happy in their doom,
For P. has wrote upon their tomb.

Epitaph written by the poet H. J. Daniel for himself:
Here lies a bard, let epitaphs be true,
His vices many, and his virtues few;
Who always left religion in the lurch
But never left a tavern for a church,
Drank more from pewter than Pierian spring
And only in his cups was known to sing;
Laugh'd at the world, however it may blame,
And died regardless of his fate or fame.

Epitaph for the wife:
To follow you I'm not content.
How do I know which way you went?

Epitaph written by Alexander Pope for himself:
Under this marble, or under the sill,
Or under this turf, or e'en what they will;
Whatever an heir, or a friend in his stead,
Or any good creature shall lay o'er my head;
Lies he who ne'er car'd, and still cares not a pin,
What they said, or may say of the mortal within.
But who living and dying, serene still and free,
Trusts in God, that as well as he was, he shall be.

Epitaph on a carrier who died of drunkenness, by Byron:
John Adams lies here, of the parish of Southwell,
A carrier who carried his can to his mouth well;
He carried so much and he carried so fast,
He could carry no more—so was carried at last;
For the liquor he drank, being too much for one,
He could not carry off; so he's now carry on.

Epitaph on Sir John Vanbrugh, English dramatist and architect:
Under this stone, reader, survey
Dead Sir John Vanbrugh's house of clay.
Lie heavy on him, earth! for he
Laid many heavy loads on thee!

Epitaph written by the banker Abraham Newland for himself:
Beneath this stone old Abraham lies;
Nobody laughs and nobody cries.
Where he is gone and how he fares
Nobody knows, and nobody cares.

Epitaph—Anonymous:
Here lies Pat Steel,
That's very true.
Who was he? what was he?
What is that to you?

Epitaph written by Abel Evans the epigrammist for himself:
Here lies the author of the 'Apparition',
Who died, God wot, but in poor condition;
If, reader, you would shun his fate,
Nor write, nor preach for Church or State,
Be dull, exceeding dull, and you'll be great.

Epitaph for a great sleeper:
Here lies a great sleeper, as everybody knows,
Whose soul would not care if his body ne'er rose,
The business of life he hated, and chose
To die for his ease for his better repose;
And 'tis believed, when the last trump doth wake him,
Had the Devil a bed, he would pray him to take him.

Epitaph on one Richard Button:
Oh! Sun, Moon, Stars, and ye celestial poles!
Are graves then dwindled into Buttonholes.

Epitaph on John Knott:
Here lies John Knott:
His father was not before him,
He lived Knott, died Knott,
Yet underneath this stone doth lie
Knott christened, Knott begot,
And here he lies and still is Knott.

Epitaph for one of the maids of honour of Queen Elizabeth I:
Here lies, the Lord have mercy upon her,
One of her Majesty's maids of honour:
She was both young, slender and pretty,
She died a maid, the more the pity.

Epitaph on Lord Coningsby, by Alexander Pope:
Here lies Lord Coningsby—be civil,
The rest God knows—so does the Devil.

Epitaph on Dr. Samuel Johnson, by Soame Jenyns:
Here lies poor Johnson. Reader! have a care,
Tread lightly, lest you rouse a sleeping bear.
Religious, moral, gen'rous and humane,
He was, but self-conceited, rude, and vain:
Ill-bred, and overbearing in dispute,
A scholar and a Christian, yet a brute.
Would you know all his wisdom and his folly,
His actions, sayings, mirth, and melancholy,
Boswell and Thrale, retailers of his wit,
Will tell you how he wrote, and talk'd, and spit.

Epitaph on a historian:
Misplacing—mistaking—
Misquoting—misdating—
Men, manners, things, facts all,
Here lies Nathan Wraxall.

Epitaph written for himself by Samuel Taylor Coleridge:
Here sleeps at length poor Col., and without screaming;
Who died as he lived, a-dreaming:
Shot dead, while sleeping, by the gout within—
All alone and unknown, at Edinbro' in an inn.

Epitaph for one Peter Robinson:
Here lies the preacher, judge, and poet, Peter
Who broke the laws of God, and man, and metre.

Epitaph for an apathetic couple, by Matthew Prior:
Interr'd beneath this marble stone
Lie Saunt'ring Jack and Idle Joan,
While rolling threescore years and one
Did round this globe their courses run;
If human things went ill or well;
If changing empires rose or fell;
The morning past, the evening came,
And found this couple still the same.
They walk'd and eat, good folks: What then?
Why then they walk'd and eat again:
They soundly slept the night away:
They did just nothing all the day:
And having buried children four,
Would not take pains to try for more.
Nor sister either had nor brother:
They seemed just tallied for each other.

Their moral and economy
Most perfectly they made agree:
Each virtue kept its proper bound,
Nor trespass'd on the other's ground.
Nor fame, nor censure they regarded:
They neither punished, nor rewarded.
He car'd not what the footmen did:
Her maids she neither prais'd, nor chid:
So ev'ry servant took his course;
And bad at first, they all grew worse.
Slothful disorder filled his stable;
And sluttish plenty decked her table.
Their beer was strong; their wine was port;
Their meal was large; their grace was short.
They gave the poor the remnant-meat,
Just when it grew not fit to eat.

They paid the church and parish rate;
And took, but read not the receipt:
For which they claimed their Sunday's due,
Of slumb'ring in an upper pew.

No man's defects sought they to know;
So never made themselves a foe.
No man's good deeds did they commend;
So never rais'd themselves a friend.

Nor cherish'd they relations poor:
That might decrease their present store:
Nor barn nor house did they repair:
That might oblige their future heir.

They neither added, nor confounded:
They neither wanted, nor abounded.

Each Christmas they accompts did clear;
And wound their bottom round the year.
Nor tear nor smile they did imploy
At news of public grief, or joy.

When bells were rung, and bonfires made,
If ask'd, they ne'er denied their aid:
Their jug was to the ringers carried.
Whoever either died, or married.
Their billet at the fire was found,
Whoever was depos'd, or crown'd.

Nor good, nor bad, nor fools, nor wise,
They would not learn, nor could advise:
Without love, hatred, joy, or fear,
They led—a kind of—as it were:
Nor wish'd, nor car'd, nor laugh'd, nor cried:
And so they liv'd; and so they died.

Epitaph on a wife:
Here lies my wife, a sad slattern and a shrew.
If I said I regretted her, I should lie too.

Epitaph on a poet:
Here lies a poet—where's the great surprise!
Since all men know, a poet deals in lies.
His patrons know, they don't deserve his praise:
He knows, he never meant it in his lays:
Knows, where he promises, he never pays.
Verse stands for sack, his knowledge for the score;
Both out, he's gone—where poets went before:
And at departing, let the waiters know
He'd pay his reck'ning in the realms below.

Epitaph for a man who died of natural causes after several suicide attempts:
He died an honest death.

Epitaph for a housewife:
Here lies a poor woman who always was tired,
She lived in a house where no help was hired.
The last words she said were "Dear Friends, I am going,
Where washing ain't wanted, nor mending, nor sewing.
There all things is done just exact to my wishes,
For where folk don't eat there's no washing of dishes.
In Heaven loud anthems for ever are ringing,
But having no voice, I'll keep clear of the singing.
Don't mourn for me now, don't mourn for me never;
I'm going to do nothing for ever and ever."

Epitaph on a lawyer:
Beneath this smooth stone by the bone of his bone
Sleeps Master John Gill;
By lies when alive this attorney did thrive,
And now that he's dead he lies still.

Epitaph on a contentious companion:
Here lies the man who in life
With every man had law and strife;
But now he's dead and laid in grave,
His bones no quiet rest can have,
For lay your ear unto this stone,
And you shall hear how every bone
Doth knock and beat against the other,
Pray for his soul's health, gentle brother.

Epitaph for a man buried with his four wives:
An excellent husband was Mr. Danner,
He lived in a thoroughly honourable manner,
He may have had troubles,
But they burst like bubbles,
He's at peace now, with Mary,
Jane, Susan and Hannah.

Epitaph for a loving husband, by his widow:
Rest in peace—until we meet again.

Epitaph on a miser:
Here lies old Forty-Five per Cent;
The more he got the more he lent,
The more he saved, the more he craved:
Great God! can such a soul be saved?

Epitaph for a bone collector:
Here lies the body of William Jones
Who all his life collected bones,
Till Death, that grim and bony spectre,
That universal bone collector,
Boned old Jones, so neat and tidy,
And here he lies, all bona fide.

Epitaph for the lawyer Sir John Strange:
Here lies an honest lawyer,
And that is Strange.

Epitaph for a famous beer drinker.
Beneath these stones repose the bones
Of Theodosius Grim;
He took his beer from year to year,
And then the bier took him.

Epitaph for a suicide:
Here lies Sir John Plumpudding of the Grange,
Who hanged himself one morning for a change.

Epitaph for an 18th century English alderman:
That he was born it cannot be denied;
He ate, slept, talk'd politics, and died.

Epitaph for an orator:
Here, reader, turn your weeping eyes,
My fate a useful moral teaches;
The hole in which my body lies
Would not contain one-half my speeches.

Epitaph on a fighter:
Strong and athletic was my frame
Far away from home I came,
And manly fought with Simon Byrnne
Alas! but lived not to return.
Reader, take warning by my fate,
Unless you rue your case too late;
And if you've ever fought before,
Determine now to fight no more.

Epitaph for a gravedigger:
I, that have carried a hundred bodies brave,
Am by a fever carried to my grave;
I carried, and am carried, so that's even;
May I be porter to the gates of heaven.

Epitaph for a blacksmith:
My sledge and anvil lie declined,
My bellows too have lost their wind;

My fire's extinct, my forge decay'd,
And in the dust my body's laid:
My coal is out, my iron's gone,
My nails are drove, my work is done.

Epitaph for an organist called Merideth:
Here lies one blown out of breath,
Who lived a merry life, and died a Merideth.

Epitaph on a two-week old baby:
Came in
Looked about
Didn't like it
Went out

Epitaph to a tight-rope walker:
Let this small monument record the name
Of Cadman, and to future times proclaim
How, by an attempt to fly from this high spire,
Across the Sabrine stream, he did acquire
His fatal end. 'Twas not for want of skill,
Or courage to perform the task, he fell;
No, no! A faulty cord drawn too tight
Hurried his soul on high to take her flight
Which bid the body here beneath, good night.

Epitaph for an old soldier:
Though shot and shell around flew fast
On Balaclava's plain,
Unscathed he passed to fall at last,
Run over by a train.

Epitaph for a pig-killer:
Here lies John Higgs,
A famous man for killing pigs,
For killing pigs was his delight
Both morning, afternoon and night.
Both heats and cold he did endure,
Which no physician could ere cure.
His knife is laid, his work is done;
I hope to heaven his soul is gone.

Epitaph to a safe-breaker:
Unknown man shot in
the Jennison & Gallup Co's store
while in the act of burglarizing
the safe Oct. 13, 1905
(Stone bought with money
found on his person)

Epitaph for a soldier, buried in Crimea:
Here lies an old soldier, whom all must applaud:
He found many battles both at home and abroad,
But the fiercest engagement he ever was in,
Was the battle of self in the conquest of sin.

Epitaph on Elihu Yale, founder of Yale University:
Born in America in Europe bred,
In Africa traveled and in Asia wed
Where long he lived and thrived. In London dead.
Much good, some ill he did, so hope all's even,
And that his soul through mercy's gone to heaven.
You that survive and read this tale take care,
For this most certain exit to prepare
Where blest in peace the actions of the just
Smell sweet and blossom in the silent dust.

Epitaph on one Stephen Remnant:
Here's a remnant of life, and a remnant of death,
Taken off at once in a remnant of breath.
To mortality this gives a happy release,
For what was the remnant proves now the whole piece.

Epitaph written by the English dramatist John Gay, for himself:
Life is a jest, and all things show it.
I thought so once; but now I know it.

Epitaph for a ragman:
I in my time did gather rags
And many a time fill'd my bags,
Altho' it was a ragged trade
My rags are sold and debts are paid.
Therefore go on and don't waste time
On bad biography and bitter rhyme,
For what I am this cumbrous clay assures
And what I was is no affair of yours.

Epitaph for a suffocated child:
Under this marble faire
Lies the body entombed of Gervaise Aire:
He died not of an ague fit,
Nor surfeited with too much wit,
Methinks this was a wonderous death
That Aire should die for want of breath.

Epitaph on a lawyer:
Robert Lives Esq. a barrister, so great a lover of peace
that when a contention arose between Life and Death he immediately yielded up the Ghost to end the dispute.

Epitaph for Dr. William Rothwell, famous Rhode Island wit and host:
This is on me . . .

Epitaph for a bellows-maker:
Here lies Robert Wallis,
Clerk of All Hallows,
King of good fellows
And maker of bellows.
He bellows did make to the day of his death,
But he that made bellows could never make breath.

Epitaph on one James Albery, written by himself:
He slept beneath the moon,
He basked beneath the sun;
He lived a life of going-to-do,
And died with nothing done.

Epitaph on the leg of the Marquis of Anglesey, buried at Waterloo, where he lost it during the battle in 1815:
Here rests—and let no saucy knave
Presume to sneer and laugh,
To learn that mouldering in the grave
Is laid—a British calf.

A leg and foot, to speak more plain
Rest here of one commanding
Who though his wits he may retain
Lost half his understanding.

And now in England, just as gay
As in the battle brave,
He goes to rout, review and play,
With one foot in the grave.

Epitaph on a sprinter:
Here lies a swift racer, so famed for his running,
In spite of his boasting, his swiftness, and cunning,
In leaping o'er ditches, and skipping o'er fields,
Death soon overtook him, and tript up his heels!

Epitaph for a priest:
Hurrah boys at the parson's fall,
For if he'd lived he'd a buried us all.

Epitaph on one William Pepper:
Tho' hot my name, yet mild my nature,
I bore good will to every creature;
I brew'd good ale and sold it too,
And unto each I gave his due.

Epitaph for a criminal:
As nurses strive their babes in bed to hie,
When they too liberally the wanton play;
So to prevent his future grievous crimes,
Nature, his nurse, got him to bed betimes.

Epitaph for an invalid:
His illness laid not in one spot,
But through his frame it spread,
The fatal disease was in his heart,
And water in his head.

Epitaph said to have been chosen by William Shakespeare for his own grave:
Good friend, for Jesus' sake forbear
To dig the dust enclosed here.
Blest be the man that spares these stones,
And curst be he that moves my bones.

Epitaph for the wife of a parish clerk:
The children of Israel wanted bread,
And the Lord he sent them manna,
Old clerk Wallace wanted a wife,
And the Devil sent him Anna.

Epitaph on one Dr. Lively:
He prolonged the lives of others to lament his own dissolution.

Epitaph for a baker:
Like to the baker's oven is the grave,
Wherein the bodyes of the faithful have
A setting in and where they do remain,
In hopes to rise, and to be drawn again!
Blessed are they who in the Lord are dead;
Though set like dough,
They shall be drawn like bread!

Epitaph for a man who died at the age of ninety:
Of no distemper
Of no blast he died,
But fell,
Like autumn fruit
That's mellowed long,
E'en wondered at
Because he dropped the sooner.
Providence seemed to wind him up
For four score years; yet ran he on
Nine winters more; till like a clock
Worn out with beating times
The wheels of weary life
At last stood still.

Epitaph for a farm labourer:
He plowed a straight furrow.

Epitaph on the English statesman Robert Lowe, by himself:
Here lies the body of Robert Lowe,
Where he's gone to, I don't know.
If to the realms of peace and love,
Farewell to happiness above!
If haply to some lower level,
I can't congratulate the Devil!

Epitaph for a dog:
Be comforted, little dog and know that at the
Resurrection you too shall have a golden tail.

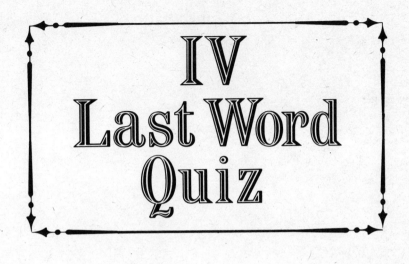

IV
Last Word
Quiz

Here are a hundred questions about the Last Words of the great, the near-great and the merely notorious. You will find the answers at the back of the book.

1. "Morituri te salutant" ("Those about to die salute you"), was the cry of which ancient combatants before they fought? Were they:
   Caesar's legions in Gaul?
   Gladiators?
   The Praetorian Guard?
   Hannibal's mercenary forces?

2. Always conscious of politeness and gentility to his subjects, he said this on his deathbed: "I fear, gentlemen, I am an unconscionable time a-dying." Which English king was he?
   George I?
   James II?
   Charles II?
   William IV?

3. Beside whose deathbed did Edwin M. Stanton say: "Now he belongs to the ages." Was it:
   Abraham Lincoln?
   Stephen A. Douglas?
   George McClellan?
   Ulysses S. Grant?

4. Which movie actress composed this epitaph for herself? "This is too deep for me." Was it:
   Joan Crawford?   Raquel Welch?
   Dorothy Lamour?   Hedy Lamarr?

5. An Irish patriot, shot in 1916, wrote these words in his last letter: "It is a cruel thing to die with all men understanding." Who was it:
   Michael Collins?
   Patrick Feaney?
   Roger Casement?
   Charles Stewart Parnell?

6. Sinking in 1912 this was her last S.O.S.: "Have struck iceberg. Badly damaged. Rush aid." Which ship was she:
   The *Lusitania?*   The *Titanic?*
   The *Mauretania?*   The *Paris?*

7. "If someone is going to kill me, they will kill me," he said, and the foreboding proved to be correct. Which President was he:
   James Garfield?
   William McKinley?
   John F. Kennedy?
   Warren G. Harding?

8. Which ancient king complained on his deathbed: "I am dying with the help of too many physicians." Was it:
   Alexander the Great?
   Herod?
   Cyrus the Great?
   Pericles?

9. "Don't judge me too harshly" was the final cable sent by rock musician Brian Jones before his death. Which band did he play for?

   The Animals?   The Rolling Stones?

   Manfred Mann?   The Cream?

10. "The rest is silence." These are the final words of which 17th century tragic hero:

    Faustus?   King Lear?

    Hamlet?   Tamburlaine?

11. In 1972 a movie tycoon said this during his last public statement: ". . . for one thing I would like to see an accurate story of my life printed." Who was it:

    Howard Hughes?

    Robert Goldstein?

    Louis B. Mayer?

    Samuel Goldwyn?

12. She left a note to her maid Lena, shortly before dying in bed: "It is 5:30 and I have been working all night. I am going to bed. Good morning." Who was she:

    Emily Dickinson?

    Edna St. Vincent Millay?

    Dorothy Parker?

    Lillie Langtry?

13. On finding the means of her suicide in a bowl of fruit, Cleopatra exclaimed: "So here it is!" To what was she referring:

    A dagger?

    An asp?

    A vial of poison?

    A scorpion?

14. Facing death, one of Dickens's characters speaks the memorable lines: "It is a far, far better thing that I do than I have ever done; it is a far, far better rest that I go to than I have ever known." In which novel does this character appear. Is it:

    Oliver Twist?
    Little Dorrit?
    Martin Chuzzlewit?
    A Tale of Two Cities?

15. Which classical poet referred to death as: "The last limit of all things." Was it:

    Homer?   Catullus?
    Horace?   Virgil?

16. The inscription on her gravestone reads:
    "Shed not for her a bitter tear
    Nor give the heart to vain regret.
    'Tis but the casket that lies here,
    The gem that fills it sparkles yet."
    Who was she:

    Belle Starr?
    Bonnie Parker?
    Annie Oakley?
    Catherine Ballou?

17. The final words of his autobiography *Stay of Execution* read: "There is a time to live, but there is also a time to die. That time has not yet come for me. But it will. It will come for all of us." Was he:

    Stewart Alsop?
    H. L. Mencken?
    James T. Farrell?
    John Sharp Williams?

18. "Top of the world, Ma!" are the last words of actor James Cagney in one of his most successful movies. Which movie is it:

    Public Enemy?
    The Roaring Twenties?
    White Heat?
    Man of a Thousand Faces?

19. He died after sending this cable to his family. His wife, who had the same name as Cleopatra's maid, wrote his biography. The cable read: "I leave California Wednesday following. Daddy." Who was the sender:

    John Steinbeck?
    Jack London?
    Clarence E. Mulford?
    Edward E. Hale?

20. Which of Shakespeare's kings exclaims these desperate last words: "A horse! A horse! my kingdom for a horse."

    Richard II?
    King John?
    Richard III?
    Henry IV?

21. What was the woman's name that Sherlock Holmes allegedly murmured on his deathbed? Was it:

    Rachel?
    Irene?
    Victoria?
    Alexandria?

22. In an interview not long before she died, she said: "I'm not afraid to die, honey. In fact I'm kind of looking forward to it. I know that the Lord has his arms

wrapped around this big, fat sparrow." Who was the 'big fat sparrow'? Was it:
    Ethel Waters?
    Flora Mae King Jackson?
    Pearl Washington?
    Ida Maitland?

23. Which novelist wrote this deathbed memorandum: "Death, the only immortal, who treats us all alike, whose peace and whose refuge are for all. The soiled and the pure, the rich and the poor, the loved and the unloved." Was it:
    William Faulkner?
    F. Scott Fitzgerald?
    Henry James?
    Mark Twain?

24. Red Skelton supplied what would have been a very apt epitaph for himself as he watched the crowds at a big funeral: "It proves what they say: give the public what they want to see and they'll come for it." Who was being buried? Was it:
    Harry Cohn?
    Irving Thalberg?
    Spyros Skouras?
    Louis B. Mayer?

25. Before being massacred by government troops in St. Petersburg, these 19th century revolutionaries cried aloud: "Yes, we shall die, but it will be a fine death." What were they called? Was it:
    The Chartists?   The Decembrists?
    The Boxers?   The Thousand Heroes?

26. Commenting on his life, this President said: "There is an epitaph in Boot Hill cemetery in Arizona which reads 'Here lies Jack Williams—he done his damndest. What more can a person do?' Well, that's all I could do. I did my damndest and that's all there is to it." Who was he:

  Franklin D. Roosevelt?
  Harry S. Truman?
  John Tyler?
  William Howard Taft?

27. Which movie actor chose this epitaph for himself, though it was never actually used: "Back to the silents."

  Charlie Chaplin?   Clark Gable?
  Oliver Hardy?   Harpo Marx?

28. Despite her success as a novelist of great influence, she felt compelled to end her life and left this suicide note: "I have a feeling I shall go mad. I cannot go on any longer in these terrible times. I hear voices and cannot concentrate on my work. I have fought against it but cannot fight any longer. I owe all my happiness to you, but cannot go on and spoil your life." Who was she:

  George Eliot?   Gertrude Stein?
  Virginia Woolf?   George Sand?

29. "LUNCH TUESDAY WET OR FINE COTTAGE ONE MILE BOVINGTON CAMP—SHAW," the last cable of an enigmatic Englishman, who was using Shaw as a pseudonym. What was his real identity? Was he:

  George Orwell?   H. H. Munro?
  T. E. Lawrence?   D. H. Lawrence?

30. "Ah, stay, thou art so fair." A German romantic poet gave these dying words to the man who is the subject of fifty-three operas and the tragic hero of a leading Elizabethan playwright: Who was the German poet? Was it:

Friedrich von Schlegel?
Johann Wolfgang von Goethe?
Thomas Mann?
Johann Christoph Friedrich von Schiller?

31. At the end of the movie the main character lies dead and this is his epitaph, spoken by Robert Armstrong: "No, it wasn't the airplane . . . it was Beauty killed the Beast." Who was the "Beast"? Was it:

Quasimodo?   King Kong?
Frankenstein?   The Mummy?

32. Which of the young men in Shakespeare's *Romeo and Juliet* dies with this curse on his lips: "A plague o'both your houses! They have made worms meat of me: I have it, And soundly too: your houses!" Is it:

Mercutio?
Tybalt?
Romeo?
Paris?

33. To whom did Harry Hopkins address this final letter: "Do give my love to Clemmie and Sarah, all of whom I shall hope to see before you go back, but I want to have a good talk with you over the state of world affairs, to say nothing of our private lives." Was it:

Franklin D. Roosevelt?   Charles De Gaulle?
Winston Churchill?   Dwight D. Eisenhower?

34. Asked to select his own epitaph, W. C. Fields suggested: "On the whole I'd rather be in—." Where would he rather have been:
    Hell?
    Hollywood?
    Pittsburgh?
    Philadelphia?

35. To her husband and her king, Henry VIII, she made this final appeal in 1536: "From a private station you have raised me to that of a countess, from a countess you have made me queen, and now you can raise me one step higher—to be a saint in heaven." Who was she:
    Catherine Howard?
    Anne Boleyn?
    Jane Seymour?
    Catherine of Aragon?

36. "One day you'll read about it:—A Suicide at 35." This message given at his last concert proved to be true in the end. Who was he:
    Phil Ochs?
    Brian Jones?
    Gram Parsons?
    Jimi Hendrix?

37. Which New Testament figure died after these final words: "I have sinned in that I have betrayed the innocent blood"?
    Pontius Pilate?
    Herod?
    Judas Iscariot?
    St. Thomas?

38. Clark Gable died soon after shooting a movie. These are the last words he spoke on camera: Asked "How do you find the way back in the dark?" he replied, with symbolic irony: "Just head for the big star straight on. The highways under it take us right home." What was the movie:

Run Silent Run Deep?   *The Misfits?*
But Not For Me?   *It Started in Naples?*

39. "I Edward VIII, of Great Britain, Ireland, and the British Dominions beyond the seas, King, Emperor of India, do hereby declare My irrecoverable determination to renounce the throne for Myself and My descendants and My desire that effect should be given to this instrument of Abdication immediately. In token whereof I have hereunto set My hand this 10th day of December 1936, in the presence of witnesses whose signatures are subscribed." The final words of a king, but who did he become:

The Duke of Kent?   The Duke of Windsor?
The Duke of Bahamas?   The Duke of London?

40. He once said that he would like his epitaph to read: "He was an average guy who could carry a tune." Who was he:

Louis Armstrong?
Enrico Caruso?
Buddy Holly?
Bing Crosby?

41. The last verse of the final poem written by bank robber Bonnie Parker reads:
"Some day they will go down together
And they will bury them side by side

To few it means grief
To the law it's relief
But it's death to Bonnie and Clyde."
Who read the poem and played the part of its writer
in the 1967 movie *Bonnie and Clyde?* Was it:

Faye Dunaway?
Jane Fonda?
Joanne Woodward?
Liza Minnelli?

42. Which fighter of the American Revolution made this
observation on the inevitability of death: "What do
you expect? Life is like the flame of a lamp—when there
is no more oil . . . zest! It goes out and all is over"?
Was it:

John Paul Jones?
Paul Revere?
George Washington?
Marquis de Lafayette?

43. During his final public lecture he said: "My doctors
East ordered a rest of brain, but you see I do not have
to work my brain for a simple lecture—it comes spon-
taneously." Who was he:

Josh Billings?
Burton Holmes?
Henry Wheeler Shaw?
Joel Chandler Harris?

44. The last words of one of the world's richest men were:
"I want my lunch." Who was he:

J. Paul Getty?   Howard Hughes?
John D. Rockefeller?   J. Pierpont Morgan?

45. These are the last words of which fictional detective: "Cher ami . . . They were good days. Yes, they were good days."

    Jacques Clouseau?   Jacques Dreyfuss?
    Inspector Maigret?   Hercule Poirot?

46. Which poet was recalling his father's last words when he said: "He said he was dying of fast women, slow horses, crooked cards and straight whiskey."? Was it:

    T. S. Eliot?   Randall Jarrell?
    Kenneth Rexroth?   e. e. cummings?

47. On the day of his execution he said to a friend, referring to King Henry VIII of England: "Had I served God as diligently as I have served the king, He would not have given me over in my grey hairs." Who was he:

    Cardinal Wolsey?   Archbishop Cranmer?
    Sir Thomas More?   Archbishop Laud?

48. He used to boast: "The bullet hasn't been made that can kill me." He was proved wrong in 1931. Who was he:

    Roger "Terrible" Touhy?
    Jack "Legs" Diamond?
    Charles "Lucky" Luciano?
    Arnold Rothstein?

49. Which President suggested this as his own epitaph: "Here lies—who took upon himself the responsibility of peace with France in the year 1800"? Was it:

    Thomas Jefferson?
    John Adams?
    James Madison?
    George Washington?

50. She asked her friend, Beatrice Ames, this question a few days before she died: "I want you to tell me the truth. Did Ernest (Hemingway) really like me?" Who was she?

Gertrude Stein?
Eleanor Roosevelt?
Dorothy Parker?
Judy Garland?

51. Before committing suicide in 1948, she wrote this note to her mother: "Dearest Mommie. I'm sorry, really sorry to put you through this. But there is no way to avoid it. I love you darling. You have been the most wonderful Mom ever. And that applies to all our family. I love each and every one of them dearly. Everything goes to you. Look in the files and there is a will which decrees everything. Goodbye my angel. Pray for me." Who was she:

Lupe Velez?
Marilyn Monroe?
Clara Bow?
Carole Landis?

52. Which French writer concluded his will: "I have nothing. I owe much. The rest I leave to the poor"? Was it:

Albert Camus?
François Rabelais?
Guy de Maupassant?
Jean de la Fontaine?

53. "I am ready to meet my Maker. Whether my Maker is prepared for the ordeal of meeting me is another matter." Who said this on his 75th birthday:

George Bernard Shaw?   Mark Twain?
Winston Churchill?   James Whistler?

54. He once chose this as his epitaph: "Pardon me for not getting up." Who was he:
    Ernest Hemingway?
    Noel Coward?
    Groucho Marx?
    Stan Laurel?

55. Talking a short time before the automobile crash in which he was killed, he said: "My fun days are over." Who made that prophetic statement:
    James Dean?
    Albert Camus?
    Buddy Holly?
    Mark Bolan?

56. "Just before she died she asked, 'What is the answer?' No answer came. She laughed and said, 'In that case, what is the question?'" Whose last words are being recalled:
    George Sand?
    Colette?
    Gertrude Stein?
    Emily Brontë?

57. His adjutant wrote down his last order, but it was too late: "Benteen—come on—Big Village—be quick—bring packs." Who was the commander:
    W. Barrett Travis?
    Henry Ward Camp?
    Lewis Benedict?
    George Custer?

58. On his 58th birthday, he had this to say about death: "At least one knows that death will be easy. A slight knock at the window pane, then . . ." Was it:
    Friedrich Wilhelm Nietzsche?
    Bertolt Brecht?
    Jean Paul Sartre?
    Ludwig Josef Johann Wittgenstein?

59. Who was this diarist whose last entry referred to the epidemic which eventually took his life: "Deaths today —sixty-six." Was it:
    John Evelyn?
    Samuel Pepys?
    Jacob Hiltzheimer?
    Gustav Mahler?

60. "Mother of Mercy . . . is this the end of Rico?" is the famous last line of which gangster movie:
    Public Enemy?
    Scarface?
    Quick Millions?
    Little Caesar?

61. Originator of a new style of music, he died in poverty with this note in his pocket: "Dear friends and gentle hearts." Who was he:
    Stephen Foster?
    George Gershwin?
    Scott Joplin?
    Duke Ellington?

62. Which movie star suggested this as an appropriate epitaph for her own tombstone:

"Of this quiet and peace
I'm very fond;
No more remarks—
She's a platinum blonde."
Was it:
    Veronica Lake?
    Jean Harlow?
    Glenda Farrell?
    Pearl White?

63. Which Irish patriot predicted his death when he commented, signing the Irish Peace Treaty: "I am signing my own death warrant."
    Eamon de Valéra?
    Roger Casement?
    Michael Collins?
    Charles Stewart Parnell?

64. The announcement of his abdication in 1917 brought about fundamental changes, not only for his own country but for the world at large: "We have recognized that it is for the good of the country that we should abdicate the Crown of ——, and lay down the supreme power." Which monarch was this:
    The last Ottoman sultan?
    The last Manchu emperor?
    Tsar Alexander II of Russia?
    Tsar Nicholas II of Russia?

65. "Die? I should say not, dear fellow. No_____ would ever allow such a conventional thing to happen to him." Who was it who said this:
    Lord Palmerston?   Benjamin Disraeli?
    John Barrymore?   Wyatt Earp?

66. Once asked to word her own epitaph she suggested: "Excuse my dust." Was she:
    Simone de Beauvoir?
    Kathleen Ferrier?
    Dorothy Parker?
    Agnes MacPhail?

67. Describing her death, her maid Charmion said that this queen of the ancient world died: "Extremely well, and as became the descendant of many kings." Whose death was she describing:
    Boadicea's?   Herodias's?
    Dido's?   Cleopatra's?

68. Invited by a fan magazine to compose his own epitaph, this movie star of both silents and talkies decided on: "Did you hear about my operation?" Who was he:
    Buster Keaton?
    Edgar Kennedy?
    Charlie Chaplin?
    Warner Baxter?

69. In which of Franz Kafka's novels does the principal character die at the end, saying: "Like a dog!" Is it:
    The Trial?
    America?
    The Castle?
    Metamorphosis?

70. "This was the noblest Roman of them all:
    All the conspirators save only he
    Did that they did in envy of great Caesar;
    He, only in a general honest thought

And common good for all made one of them.
His life was gentle, and the elements
So mix'd in him that Nature might stand up
And say to all the world, 'This was a man!' "
Over whose body does Mark Antony speak these lines
at the end of Shakespeare's tragedy *Julius Caesar?* Is it
the body of:

    Cassius?   Brutus?

    Casca?   Cinna?

71. She suggested this for her own epitaph: "Do not disturb." Who was she:

    Constance Bennett?

    Emily Dickinson?

    Sylvia Plath?

    Eleanor Roosevelt?

72. He was a mass murderer who left this note before turning his gun on himself in the tower of Texas State University: "Life is not worth living." Who was he:

    Son of Sam?

    The Boston Strangler?

    Charles Starkweather?

    Charles Whitman?

73. In 1973 he announced to the world: "The industrial nations will have to realize this era of terrific progress and even more terrific wealth based on cheap oil is finished." Who was it heralding the world recession:

    Mu'ammer al-Quadhafi?

    The Shah of Iran?

    King Faisal?

    Dr. Henry Kissinger?

74. The final entry in his notebook reads: "At fifty every-one has the face that he deserves." Which British writer jotted these words:

> George Orwell?
> P. G. Wodehouse?
> G. K. Chesterton?
> Eric Blair?

75. A big Hollywood star of the thirties, he composed these telling lines as his own epitaph:
"Here in nature's arms I nestle,
Free at last from Georgie Jessel."
Who was he:

> George Arliss?
> Al Jolson?
> George Jessel?
> Eddie Cantor?

76. Which movie star left this suicide note in 1944: "To Harald, May God forgive you and forgive me too but I prefer to take my life away and our baby's before I bring him with shame or killing him,—" On the back it read: "How could you, Harald, fake such a great love for me and our baby when all the time you didn't want us. I see no other way out for me so goodbye and good luck to you. Love—." Was it:

> Marilyn Monroe?
> Lupe Velez?
> Judy Garland?
> Angela Delgado?

77. Asked on one occasion how he would like his epitaph to read, he suggested: "Here's something I want to get off my chest." Was he:
   Bud Abbott?
   Roscoe Fatty Arbuckle?
   Lou Costello?
   William Haines?

78. This late Victorian and Edwardian British actress wrote this final word in the dust on the table beside her bed: "Happy." Who was she:
   Sarah Bernhardt?
   Lillie Langtry?
   Ellen Terry?
   Mrs. Patrick Campbell?

79. "If, after I depart this vale, you remember me and have some thought to please my ghost, forgive some sinner and wink your eye at some homely girl." Which critic and social commentator wrote this epitaph for himself:
   Mark Twain?
   H. L. Mencken?
   Ogden Nash?
   Ralph Waldo Emerson?

80. "I wanted to be an up-to-date King. But I didn't have much time." Which King said this:
   King Constantine II of Greece?
   King Edward VIII of England?
   King Michael of Rumania?
   King Zog I of Albania?

81. Which poetess wrote this poem of farewell to her daughter:
"For it is not right that in the house of song
there be mourning. Such things befit not us."
> Marianne Moore?
> Amy Lowell?
> Christina Rossetti?
> Sappho?

82. To her husband she wrote what was to be her final letter, saying: "Please know that I am aware of the hazards. I want to do it. Women must try to do things as men have tried. When they fail, their failure must be but a challenge to others." Who was this brave woman:
> Amy Johnson?
> Amelia Earhart?
> Lady Jane Ellenborough?
> Mrs. Joanna Crapo?

83. At the end of the movie, the dying Lee Marvin says to Angie Dickinson: "Lady, I don't have the time." Which is the movie:
> *The Dirty Dozen?*
> *The Killers?*
> *Cat Ballou?*
> *The Professionals?*

84. Which composer sent this final cable of jubilation in 1920: "House sold out for Friday night, box office *Vox Dei* hurrah!":
> George Gershwin?   Charles Ives?
> Reginald de Koven?   Frederick Delius?

85. A leading Irish dramatist composed this epitaph for himself: "I knew if I stayed around long enough, something like this would happen." Who was he:
    Oscar Wilde?
    George Bernard Shaw?
    J. M. Synge?
    Sean O'Casey?

86. Dying in Africa he made this last entry in his journal: "Knocked up quite, and remain—recover sent to buy milch goats. We are on the banks of the River Molilamo." Was he:
    Mungo Park?
    Charles Wilkes?
    Richard Burton?
    David Livingstone?

87. Which of Shakespeare's characters dies with these words: "O true apothecary! Thy drugs are quick. Thus with a kiss I die." Is it:
    Romeo?
    Othello?
    Old Gobbo?
    Cymbeline?

88. Which movie star dreamed up this witty epitaph for himself: "Well, I've played everything but a harp."
    Errol Flynn?
    Lionel Barrymore?
    Clark Gable?
    Claude Raines?

89. Paul Bern killed himself two months after his marriage. He left this note to his movie star wife: "Dearest Dear,

Unfortunately this is the only way to make good the frightful wrong I have done you. And to wipe out my abject humiliation." Who was she:

    Susan Hayward?
    Mary Boland?
    Jean Harlow?
    Betty Blythe?

90. This boast cost who his life: "I fix the price of beer in this town.":

    Al Capone?
    John Doyle Lee?
    Wilbur Underhill?
    Jake Lingle?

91. Who said this farewell to his favorite retreat: "Goodbye, Matapedia.":

    Eugene A. Hoffman?
    Henry David Thoreau?
    Brigham Young?
    Stephen Foster?

92. Shortly before his death he said of his life: "I've had a hell of a lot of fun and I've enjoyed every minute of it." Who was he:

    Douglas Fairbanks?
    Errol Flynn?
    Chico Marx?
    Jack Benny?

93. "I will not resign. I declare my will to resist by every means, even at the cost of my life." Which socialist statesman made this statement that was ultimately to be proven true:

Salvador Allende? Alexander Dubček?
Mohammed Daoud? Pol Pot?

94. The champion of the cause of feminism, Catherine
    Beecher, sent this last cable in 1878: "I hope to be in——
    in about ten days. I am stronger than for years, but
    take no new responsibilities." Where did she hope to
    be:
    Boston?
    San Francisco?
    Philadelphia?
    New York?

95. Which Hollywood actor composed this modest epitaph
    for himself: "This is just my lot." Was it:
    Humphrey Bogart?
    Fredric March?
    Alan Ladd?
    Buster Keaton?

96. "You won't have Nixon to kick around any more, gentle-
    men. This is my last Press Conference." In which year
    did Richard Nixon say these famous "last words":
    1960?
    1962?
    1975?
    1977?

97. He died in bed, but not alone. This epitaph was sug-
    gested by a Hollywood wit: "Died in the saddle." Who
    was he:
    Attila the Hun?
    Felix Faure?
    John Garfield?
    Rudolph Valentino?

98. Before her contract lapsed, Clara Bow said: "I've been working hard for years and I need a rest. So I'm figuring on going to Europe for a year or more when my contract expires." Where did she actually go when the time came, and remained until her death:

Mexico?
Canada?
An asylum?
Chicago?

99. Lewis Stone selected this as an epitaph he would have liked over his grave: "A gentleman farmer goes back to the———" What did he go "back to":

"prairies"?
"wild"?
"soil"?
"range"?

100. Which Nazi leader left this final statement in 1945: "My wife and I choose to die in order to escape the shame of overthrow or capitulation. It is our wish for our bodies to be cremated immediately on the place where I have performed the greater part of my daily work during the past twelve years of my service to my people.":

Heinrich Himmler?
Adolf Hitler?
Joseph Goebbels?
Martin Bormann?

Answers

1. Gladiators
2. Charles II
3. Ulysses S. Grant
4. Hedy Lamarr
5. Roger Casement
6. The *Titanic*
7. John F. Kennedy
8. Alexander the Great
9. The Rolling Stones
10. Hamlet
11. Howard Hughes
12. Edna St. Vincent Millay
13. An asp
14. *A Tale of Two Cities*
15. Horace
16. Belle Starr
17. Stewart Alsop
18. *White Heat*
19. Jack London
20. Richard III
21. Irene
22. Ethel Waters
23. Mark Twain
24. Harry Cohn
25. The Decembrists
26. Harry S. Truman
27. Clark Gable
28. Virginia Woolf
29. T. E. Lawrence
30. Johann Wolfgang von Goethe
31. King Kong
32. Mercutio
33. Winston Churchill
34. Philadelphia
35. Anne Boleyn
36. Phil Ochs
37. Judas Iscariot
38. *The Misfits*
39. The Duke of Windsor
40. Bing Crosby
41. Faye Dunaway
42. Marquis de Lafayette
43. Josh Billings was the pseudonym of Henry Wheeler Shaw
44. J. Paul Getty
45. Hercule Poirot
46. Kenneth Rexroth
47. Cardinal Wolsey
48. Jack "Legs" Diamond
49. John Adams
50. Dorothy Parker
51. Carole Landis
52. François Rabelais
53. Winston Churchill
54. Ernest Hemingway
55. James Dean
56. Gertrude Stein
57. George Custer
58. Bertolt Brecht
59. Jacob Hiltzheimer
60. *Little Caesar*
61. Stephen Foster
62. Jean Harlow
63. Michael Collins

64. Tsar Nicholas II of Russia
65. John Barrymore
66. Dorothy Parker
67. Cleopatra's
68. Warner Baxter
69. *The Trial*
70. Brutus
71. Constance Bennett
72. Charles Whitman
73. The Shah of Iran
74. George Orwell was the pseudonym of Eric Blair
75. Eddie Cantor
76. Lupe Velez
77. William Haines
78. Ellen Terry
79. H. L. Mencken
80. King Edward VIII of England
81. Sappho
82. Amelia Earhart
83. *The Killers*
84. Reginald de Koven
85. George Bernard Shaw
86. David Livingstone
87. Romeo
88. Lionel Barrymore
89. Jean Harlow
90. Jake Lingle
91. Eugene A. Hoffman
92. Errol Flynn
93. Salvador Allende
94. Philadelphia
95. Fredric March
96. 1962
97. John Garfield
98. An asylum
99. "soil"
100. Adolf Hitler

SUBJECT INDEX